SCENIC DRIVING
WEST VIRGINIA

THIRD EDITION

SCENIC DRIVING

WEST VIRGINIA

Including Harpers Ferry, Historic Railroads, and Waterfalls

SU CLAUSON-WICKER

Guilford, Connecticut

All the information in this guidebook is subject to change. We recommend that you call ahead to obtain current information before traveling.

Globe
Pequot

An imprint of The Rowman & Littlefield Publishing Group, Inc.
4501 Forbes Blvd., Ste. 200
Lanham, MD 20706
rowman.com

Distributed by NATIONAL BOOK NETWORK

British Library Cataloguing in Publication Information available

Library of Congress Control Number: 2020950441

ISBN 978-1-4930-5826-6 (paper : alk. paper)
ISBN 978-1-4930-5827-3 (electronic)

∞™ The paper used in this publication meets the minimum requirements of American National Standard for Information Sciences—Permanence of Paper for Printed Library Materials, ANSI/NISO Z39.48-1992.

Contents

About the Author

Su Clauson-Wicker's diverse career includes a decade as editor of *Virginia Tech Magazine,* as well as positions in television, radio, medical public relations, and child welfare. She grew up in an upstate New York county often compared unfavorably to the Mountain State, attended Cornell University, and after getting her master's degree, she wasted no time in moving near the West Virginia border, to Blacksburg, Virginia. She spends nearly a month in West Virginia each year. She is author of the *Inn to Inn Walking Guide* for the Virginias, as well as the Globe Pequot Press book *West Virginia Off the Beaten Path.*

Acknowledgments

I'd like to express my indebtedness to the first author of *Scenic Driving West Virginia,* Bruce Sloane, whose knowledge and organization blazed a solid path to follow in our mutual mining of the treasures along the byways of the Mountain State. Thank you, Bruce.

I owe mountains of gratitude to my friend Estill Putney, without whose enthusiastic companionship, expert driving, adventuresome spirit, and artistic perceptions this book might never have happened in a timely fashion, and it certainly wouldn't have been half so much fun.

Without the help of scores of wonderful West Virginia people, our travels would not have been so eye-opening, rich, and enjoyable. My thanks go out to you, and may you continue to enrich the lives of future visitors. It's impossible to list everyone, but here are a few folks who have been especially helpful: Sissie Summers of West Virginia State Parks, Kari Thompson of Stonewall Group, Olivia Litman of Wheeling Convention & Visitors Bureau, Caryn Gresham and David Rotenizer of West Virginia Culture and History, Stephen Shaluta and Jacqueline Proctor of West Virginia Commerce, Rachael Stebbins of Greenbrier Convention & Visitors Bureau, Mark Lewis of Parkersburg Convention & Visitors Bureau, Mike Smith of Droop Mountain State Park, Mike Foster of Lost River State Park, Steve Jones of North Bend State Park, Ken McClintic of Holly River State Park, and my friend and fellow Milkweed writer, Cheryl Ruggiero.

I am also indebted to editor Kevin Sirois at Globe Pequot Press, who knows how to smooth the process and get things done, despite having acute appendicitis in mid-project. Last but not least, I give heartfelt gratitude to my husband, Bruce Wicker, for understanding, self-reliance, and keeping things running and everyone fed during the months I've been focused on West Virginia.

Overview

Map Legend

Interstate Highway/ Featured Interstate Highway	——(70)—— / ——(70)——
US Highway/ Featured US Highway	——(30)—— / ——(22)——
State Highway/ Featured State Highway	——(2)—— / ——(2)——
Local, Forest, County Road/ Featured Local Road	——[3]—— / ——[3]——
Unpaved Road/ Featured Unpaved Road	– – – – – – – / – – – – – – –
Trail	· · · · · · · · · · · · · · ·
Railroad	++++++++++++++++++++

Bridge	⁾⁽	Route Number	(10)
Building or Structure	■	Town	○
Campground	▲	Wildlife Management Area	⊁
Dam	—	Small State Park, Wilderness, or Natural Area	▲
Falls	⧤		
Lodge	⊨	Ski Area	⛷
Museum	🏛	Visitor, Interpretive Center	⑦
Pass	) (		
Point of Interest	◻		

Mountain, Peak, or Butte	▲ Desert Peak 11,031 ft.
River, Creek, or Drainage	～～～
Body of Water	⬭
State Line	– · – · – · – · – · –
National Forest	▢
State Forest	▢
Wilderness Area	▢
Wildlife Management Area/National River	▢

Introduction

West Virginia—"West, by God, Virginia," as they sometimes say if someone confuses their state with western Virginia. It seems appropriate to invoke the cosmic hand in forming the natural beauty of the Mountain State. The thundering New River Gorge, the high vistas of Dolly Sods, the delicate orchids of Cranberry Glades Botanical Area, the labyrinthine loveliness of Beartown State Park, or the majesty of Kanawha Falls—all within a few hours' drive—combine into the uniquely appealing and sometimes awe-inspiringly gorgeous 24,231 square miles of West Virginia. Although you will see strip mining as well as natural-gas drilling pads, you'll find that much of West Virginia is still greener, more rustic, and more relaxed than most of its more industrialized neighbors.

It's a small state, 41st in size, but within its boundaries you can find major ski resorts, sophisticated cities, ancient Indian mounds, native trout streams, arctic vegetation, Civil War battle sites, a world-class spring resort, and a state-run craft showplace, where culinary school graduates serve gourmet soups for the price of a fast-food burger. West Virginians know perfectly well—as do those of us who venture off the interstates—that the tiresome stereotypes of mountaineers are hogwash. West Virginians are about the most friendly, helpful, and unpretentious people you'll find. Most are proud to live in a state with one of the lowest crime rates and highest percentages of home ownership in the nation. They take pride in their heritage and are happy to show you why they love their land.

Classifying West Virginia, even its regionality, is difficult. The US Census Bureau classifies it as part of the South, though the Northern Panhandle extends up along Pennsylvania and Ohio, closer to both their capitals than Charleston. Bluefield, in the southeast, is less than 70 miles from North Carolina, while Martinsburg and Harpers Ferry in the Eastern Panhandle region are considered part of the Washington metropolitan area. It is the only state entirely within the area served by the Appalachian Regional Commission, the area known as Appalachia.

For geological purposes, the state is divided into two physiographic provinces. The western two-thirds lie in the Appalachian Plateau province of relatively flat-lying rocks with mineable coal. Streams dissect this area into a maze of irregular hills and valleys. West Virginia is the only state to lie almost entirely within the Appalachian Plateau.

The eastern third of the state is dominated by the northeast–southwest ridges of the Valley and Ridge province, with its intricately folded rocks, sinuous peaks,

and cavernous valleys. An exception is the extreme portion of the Eastern Panhandle near Harpers Ferry, which is an extension of the Blue Ridge Mountains and Shenandoah Valley of Virginia.

The boundary between the Valley and Ridge province and the Appalachian Plateau is the imposing Allegheny Front, which at its maximum rises 2,500 feet above the plateau and includes the highest and some of the most scenic areas of the state.

The New River, known for world-class whitewater rafting, has eroded into a 1,000-foot-deep gorge across the Allegheny Front.

The southern and southwest areas of the state contain some of the largest deposits of bituminous coal in the country. Although mining practices during the early 1900s scarred the land, recent reclamation projects have partially restored some damaged areas. In addition to bituminous coal, the state's economically important mineral deposits are abundant oil and gas, limestone, sandstone, and rock-salt beds. As mining has become more mechanized, jobs have decreased, and gradually recreation and travel are being recognized as the best use of the land.

The Ohio River forms most of the western border of the state and has been an important avenue for transportation since the first settlers. Industrial sites are common along the Ohio, but the river remains a powerful and scenic presence.

The 2018 census shows a population of 1.8 million residents. Charleston, the state capital, with 47,000 people is the largest city (except when a West Virginia University football game swells Morgantown to 75,000 souls); the Charleston metropolitan area has a population of about 200,000.

The census shows a small but steady rural movement; most larger cities and towns lost population while the rural population increased. The biggest population increase was in the Eastern Panhandle, within commuting distance of the high-tech and government jobs of northern Virginia east of Harpers Ferry.

Forests cover about three-fourths of the state, and there are approximately 2,000 miles of streams and rivers. The state's highest point is Spruce Knob with an elevation of 4,863 feet; the lowest point is the Potomac River at Harpers Ferry with an elevation of 247 feet.

At lower elevations the forests consist of red and white oak, hickory, yellow poplar, maple, black cherry, and other hardwoods. At higher elevations and on steep slopes and gorges are several species of pines, hemlock, and spruce. Logging is widespread and an important economic factor.

Virginia white-tailed deer, rabbit, squirrel, skunk, raccoon, opossum, and groundhog are common, and, in high country, black bear. Streams support

Lighthorse Harry Lee's summer house stands at Lost River State Park.

smallmouth and largemouth bass, trout, and pike; larger rivers have perch, blue-gill, catfish, and other species. Hunting and fishing are both popular recreational activities. The many varied habitats lead to abundant bird life, with more than 500 known species seen in the state.

The earliest inhabitants of the area were Paleo-Indians, or early nomadic hunters, who arrived sometime before 11,000 BC. Between 7,000 and 1,000 BC, several Archaic cultures developed in the Northern Panhandle, the Eastern Panhandle, and the Kanawha Valley. The use of gardens, pottery, and ceremonial burial mounds around 1,000 BC marked the beginning of the Adena villager culture. They were followed by the Hopewell people, who in turn were succeeded by the Native Americans of various tribes. By 1600, organized tribes such as the Delaware and Shawnee had moved into present-day West Virginia. In addition, the powerful Iroquois Confederacy exerted control over hunting rights within the region. Around 1730 the first permanent white settlers came to the area. The region was part of Virginia from the American Revolution until 1861, when the people voted not to secede with eastern Virginia. West Virginia was admitted to the US as a separate state in 1863.

Most of West Virginia enjoys four distinct seasons but with a wide range of variation. Precipitation averages 40 to 60 inches across the state. Snowfall averages 20 to 30 inches per year, except in Canaan Valley and the highest mountains, which receive 160 to 180 inches annually.

The scenic drives in this book were selected to display the most interesting scenic, historical, and unique features of diverse sections of the state. You can begin most drives at several places along the route, or tour them in reverse order. Most are over paved, two-lane roads. Note in the descriptions that a few drives travel over rough, unpaved roads, and you may decide up front not to travel there in certain seasons, or at all.

Information for each drive starts with a one-paragraph sketch of the drive, including total mileage. The main points along the drive are listed as "special attractions," which can be scenic, historical, cultural, or otherwise interesting. The section of "driving route numbers" uses this format:

- I   Interstate highway. I-79, for example. No drives follow interstates, but some drives begin at interstate exits, or an interstate is mentioned as a reference point.
- US   United States highway, such as US 119 and US 220.
- WV   West Virginia highway, for instance WV 28, WV 5-1, or WV 28/55. If the road has a name, that is shown also.

Sugar maples add fire to the autumn sky in Preston County.

- CR   County road, for instance CR 10, CR 10-4. Hyphens (-) indicate feeder roads. Slashes (/) indicate multiple route numbers for the same stretch of highway (WV 28/55).
- FS   US Forest Service route, FS 11 for example.

The text indicates if a drive is particularly attractive at a certain time of year, perhaps when seasonal waterfalls are flowing or spring redbuds are blooming. Some drives are best not attempted in winter, and this notation is made. Even on all-season drives, some attractions will not be operating year-round. "Camping" lists public and private campgrounds near the route. "Complete facilities" indicates that at least some sites have hookups, water, and indoor plumbing. The term "services" refer to the availability of gasoline, food, and lodging, and "all services" means that all three are obtainable. "Nearby attractions" lists points of interest near the drive, including other scenic routes.

It's only a slight exaggeration to say that every road in West Virginia is a scenic drive. Even the interstates are beautiful, and every road in the Monongahela, George Washington, and Jefferson National Forests is a scenic road. For some other scenic, noninterstate federal roads not included in this book, try these: US 33 between Bridgeport and Parkersburg, US 119 from Charleston to the Kentucky line, or any part of US 219 (parts of it are already on scenic drives). Enjoy your exploration!

The appendix lists phone numbers, addresses, and websites of visitor information centers and local points of interest, arranged numerically by route number.

Northern Panhandle

The Industrial Ohio River

General description: A 55-mile drive along the Ohio River bluffs in the Northern Panhandle of the state, with forays to the wooded uplands away from the river, ending in Wheeling.

Special attractions: Ohio River, Mountaineer Gaming Resort, Tomlinson Run State Park, Homer Laughlin China factory tours, Bethany College, Oglebay Resort and Conference Center, Victorian Wheeling, Wheeling Jamboree, and Wheeling Downs Race Track.

Location: Northernmost West Virginia.

Driving route numbers: WV 2, 3, 8, 67, 88, 208; OH 7 for the complete loop.

Travel season: All year. Travel is very heavy around Wheeling in November and December during Wheeling's Festival of Lights.

Camping: Tomlinson Run State Park has 54 campsites, most with complete facilities.

Services: All services are available in many towns along the drive.

Nearby attractions: Grave Creek Mound Historic Site, Old West Virginia Penitentiary, and the Palace of Gold (these are all on Scenic Route 2); Pittsburgh, Pennsylvania (40 miles east), Hillcrest Wildlife Management Area, and Castleman Run Lake Wildlife Management Area.

The Route

West Virginia's narrow Northern Panhandle juts north from the rest of the state like a raised pinky. The panhandle, only 4 miles wide in spots, is bordered by Ohio and the Ohio River on the west and Pennsylvania on the east. The only section of the state north of the Mason-Dixon Line, this north-ranging section of West Virginia is closer to Canada at its northernmost point than it is to West Virginia's own southern border.

The Northern Panhandle got its skinny shape due to pre-Revolutionary boundary disputes between Virginia and Pennsylvania. The Ohio River transportation artery has been a major influence on the area for more than 200 years. From the river's beginning at the confluence of the Allegheny and Monongahela rivers in Pittsburgh, Pennsylvania, the Ohio flows for 981 miles before merging with the Mississippi River near Cairo, Illinois. For about 275 miles, the Ohio River marks the western boundary of West Virginia.

This drive follows the Ohio River from the northern tip of West Virginia south to Wheeling. Scenic Route 3 also follows the Ohio, from New Martinsville to Parkersburg.

Before the Pleistocene ice sheets moved south, the preglacial Ohio River flowed north to empty into the ancestors of the Great Lakes. Several times during

Northern Panhandle

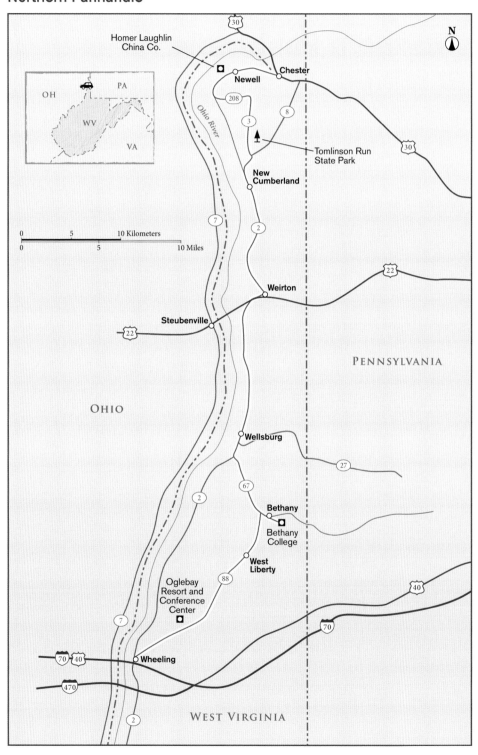

Homer Laughlin
China Co.

Newell

Chester

OH

PA

WV

VA

Ohio River

208

3

8

Tomlinson Run
State Park

New
Cumberland

7

2

30

30

0   5   10 Kilometers
0   5   10 Miles

22

Weirton

Steubenville

22

PENNSYLVANIA

OHIO

Wellsburg

27

67

2

Bethany

Bethany
College

West
Liberty

Oglebay
Resort and
Conference
Center

88

40

7

70

70   40

Wheeling

470

2

WEST VIRGINIA

N

the Pleistocene epoch, continental glaciers formed large lakes to the north, damming the Ohio and directing it on a detour south to the Gulf of Mexico. The river maintained this drainage pattern along its present course after the ice sheets melted.

The Ohio is a working river. Steel mills, coal mines, power companies, and manufacturing plants hug its banks or lie nearby. Transporters—specialized aerial conveyer belts—carry coal from hillside mine heads down to the river. There they are loaded onto mile-long barges pushed by powerful diesel tow boats that slowly work their way up and down the waterway.

A quarter mile to a half mile wide, the Ohio curves gently between verdant hills that rise several hundred feet above the river. Rocky cliffs of sandstone and limestone poke through the greenery. Fertile fields along the river support herds of cattle and patches of Queen Anne's lace. Occasional towns huddle close to the river or spread over infrequent flat areas. Graceful bridges, some new, some more than 150 years old, span the water.

In the 1700s, explorers and settlers used the Ohio as a conduit for their westward travels. It served as the starting point for Lewis and Clark's 1804 expedition. Towns sprang up, and commerce flourished along the river, though most of the surrounding territory was still forested wilderness. Local boatyards used the abundant timber to construct vessels for the westward migration down the Ohio. Farmers and traders shipped their goods downriver to New Orleans, where the boats were dismantled for their lumber.

Travel was restricted by the depth of the water, which during dry months could be less than a foot deep in shallows between Pittsburgh and Cincinnati. Shippers had to wait, sometimes months, for rain-swollen waters to carry their products downriver.

In the early 1800s the federal government began to clear and maintain the channel, but navigation was still difficult and treacherous. It wasn't until 1885 that the first lock and dam was opened, creating a navigable pool of water just below Pittsburgh. Today seven locks and dam complexes straddle the Ohio River along the Mountain State. These keep the river navigable by creating a minimum 9-foot depth year-round.

You can make this a loop drive by crossing the river to Ohio at Wheeling and following scenic four-lane OH 7 north. At East Liverpool, follow US 30 south across the river to Chester and WV 2. Turn south on this two-lane road for the main drive. The Ohio link adds about 45 miles to the drive, for a total of about 100 miles.

The World's Largest Teapot

The West Virginia portion of the drive begins in **Chester** at the intersection of WV 2 and US 30 near the **World's Largest Teapot.** This chunk of kitsch lured shoppers into a pottery outlet for almost 50 years. Rumor has it that the teapot began life as a hogshead barrel used in a root beer publicity campaign. Nevertheless, it now serves as a symbol for one of region's leading industry and the home of the largest domestic pottery factory, Homer Laughlin, just west on WV 2.

A few miles past Chester, the drive passes the well-marked entrance to the famous **Homer Laughlin China Company** (fiestafactorydirect.com), the manufacturer of Fiestaware and the main employer in Newell. The company's popular, low-cost, multihued Fiesta chinaware is used in millions of homes and restaurants. A retail store is open daily; factory tours are conducted weekday mornings.

West Virginia was a major glass-producing state beginning in the early 1800s. Glass manufacturing requires abundant supplies of silica, SiO_2, from sandstone rock, and for high-grade glass manufacturing it must be pure, at least 96 percent silica. The Oriskany sandstone, found throughout the state, meets this requirement. Today the only major quarry for Oriskany sandstone is near Berkeley Springs in the Eastern Panhandle; it is the major source of smelting sand in West Virginia and the eastern US.

By the 1830s numerous glass factories had sprung up along the Ohio River, with Wheeling as the hub, producing drinking glasses, window glass, and other products demanded by the growing country. The glassware was shipped by barges plying the Ohio River and later by railroad. When wood fuel became more scarce in the early 1900s, the natural gas deposits in the Oriskany sandstone began to play a crucial role in the glass industry.

Evidence of the glass industry is scant now as WV 2 continues south along the river, with views of 300-foot-high bluffs on both sides. After a few miles you reach the **Mountaineer Race Track and Resort** (cnty.com/mountaineer), which features live thoroughbred racing May through November plus simulcast racing from other tracks nationwide. If the horses aren't running, numerous video slots and poker machines or golf, tennis, or live concerts may hold your interest. Other amenities include several restaurants and a lodge with spa services.

Just past the resort turn left (east) on WV 208. This winding, two-lane road quickly leaves the hustle and bustle along the river as it climbs a narrow, wooded gully. After 3 miles, turn right (south) at the stop sign onto WV 3, passing through rolling countryside alternating between deciduous forests and cattle farms.

Soon you pass the entrance to **Tomlinson Run State Park** (wvstateparks.com/park/tomlinosn-run-state-park), where several short hiking trails lead past

The world's largest spot of tea symbolizes West Virginia's china industry.
WEST VIRGINIA DEPARTMENT OF COMMERCE, STEPHEN SHALUTA

overhanging cliffs of sandstone and shale. Anglers try to catch trout, bass, and catfish in the park's 33 acres of ponds. The park also has a campground, cabins, domed yurt lodging, a swimming pool, and a variety of activities. The park hosts numerous events, from car shows to pre-1840 historic encampments.

Turn right (west) on WV 8, which leads down through the Ohio River bluffs back to WV 2 at New Cumberland. Turn left (south) on WV 2. The drive continues to follow the river but climbs up the bluffs for long-range views upstream and down.

At **Weirton,** the drive passes through the **Weirton Steel Corporation** plant, which straddles both sides of the road. The town itself spans the entire state (5 miles wide at this point) from Ohio to Pennsylvania. At one point, Weirton Steel was the world's largest steel company owned by the employees. It invented the "flip top" can we use today. After years of losing money, the plant workers bought out the owners in 1984. Weirton struggled to compete with steel imports and declared bankruptcy in 2003. It has been sold twice. Blast furnaces are idled, and the ArcelorMittal Weirton steel plant now employs less than one-tenth of the 11,000 people who once worked there.

On the other side of Weirton, WV 2 joins four-lane US 22 between two exits, for about 0.75 mile. Look for the WV 2 exit to continue the drive south, following the bends in the Ohio River to the historic river town of **Wellsburg,** founded in 1791. At one time five glass companies operated kilns in the town. Brooke Hills, a park named after the last surviving glass company, offers 18-hole golf, a swimming pool, fishing, camping, and lodging cottages.

In the late 1700s the Wellsburg wharf was the loading area for flatboats heading south loaded with cargoes of glass and other freight. Only remnants of the wharf remain, including the foundations of two warehouses where goods awaiting shipment were held. However, the Wellsburg historical district features numerous restored pre-colonial and federalist buildings.

Bethany & Bethany College

Just past Wellsburg, turn left (east) on WV 67. Once more you climb up a ravine out of the Ohio River Valley to emerge amid rolling hills, woods, and well-kept farms. After about 5 miles, cross WV 88 and continue about 0.5 mile to the tree-lined streets of **Bethany,** home of **Bethany College.** The entire town is on the National Register of Historic Places.

The college, established in 1840, is the oldest private institution of higher learning in West Virginia. Although it is a small school with fewer than 1,000 students, its centerpiece, the redbrick Old Main Building, extends farther than the length of a football field. Its Gothic clock tower can be seen from almost anywhere on campus. Construction of the building began before the Civil War; it was finally finished in 1911 and renovated in the 1980s. Ask at the historic Alexander Campbell Mansion Visitor Center for tours of the college, including the Old Bethany Meeting House, built in 1850. The 1790s-era Campbell House was the home of the college founder, who was also one of the founders of the Disciples of Christ denomination.

When you leave Bethany, return to the intersection of WV 67 and WV 88 and turn left (south) on WV 88, which follows a small open ridge. The picturesque village below is **West Liberty,** home of West Liberty State College. The school was the oldest academy in West Virginia, established in 1837, and became a college a few years later. Its former president's home now serves area visitors as the Liberty Oaks Bed and Breakfast.

About 5 miles past West Liberty is the **Oglebay Resort & Conference Center** (oglebay-resort.com). Run by the Wheeling Parks Commission, this 1,600-acre public park and complex attracts more than three million visitors a year, many from abroad. Its meticulously maintained grounds, buildings, and attractions include 4 golf courses, a ski slope, 2 museums, and outstanding flower gardens.

Oglebay Park & Resort

The park got its start in 1926 when industrialist Colonel Earl Oglebay bequeathed his summer estate, 750-acre Waddington Farm, to Wheeling for public use. Today the park includes West Virginia's only accredited zoo, formal gardens, a lodge and conference center, nature center, numerous shops, a mansion, and a sports center. A large selection of West Virginia decorative glass is exhibited at the Carriage Glass House. While some attractions charge an admission fee, many are free.

The **Good Zoo,** a contribution of the Good family, is designed for children and specializes in natural North American habitats and endangered species, such as pandas and lemurs. A petting zoo gives visitors hands-on contact with friendly furries.

The **Schrader Environmental Education Nature Center** is acclaimed for its butterfly exhibit, wildflowers, interpretive nature trails, and wildlife and environmental education programs for children. It is also a regional showcase for green architecture.

Oglebay's busiest season occurs from November through December during Wheeling's **Festival of Lights,** when more than 300 acres of trees, buildings, and structures created for the occasion are adorned with energy-saving LED lights. A 6-mile drive is required to take in all this electrical bling.

Our scenic drive ends a few miles west in Wheeling at the intersection of WV 88 and US 40. Turn right (west) on US 40 to go downtown. Look for the landmark Windmill Pub building on the hill. Despite Wheeling's many attractions, most travelers see little of the city as they zoom through the Northern Panhandle on I-70.

During the 1800s, **Wheeling,** at the edge of the western frontier, was known as the Gateway to the West. The town flourished as a supply area for Ohio River travelers headed west or south. Its stately Victorian mansions, now a part of Victorian Wheeling National Historic District, are a tribute to the wealth and expert craftsmanship of the era.

Land travelers heading west left town via the graceful **Wheeling Suspension Bridge,** completed in 1849, more than 40 years before New York's famed Brooklyn Bridge. The Wheeling Suspension Bridge was overhauled and renovated in 1999 and still carries traffic between downtown and historic Wheeling Island (now home of Wheeling Island Racetrack & Gaming Center) in the Ohio River. The original toll was 10 cents for a man and horse, $1.25 for a four-horse carriage; now the National Historic Landmark is free for both pedestrians and vehicles. A waterfront park just south of the bridge allows for the best viewing. South of the riverside amphitheatre there stands a statue of Walter Reuther, Wheeling-born labor-union leader who died in 1970.

This northern city is also the birthplace of the state of West Virginia; regional leaders agreed here at **Independence Hall** (wvculture.org) to break free from the rest of Virginia and form the Reformed State of Virginia, later known as West Virginia. From 1861 to 1863, the Customs House, as Independence Hall was called then, served as the state capitol. In 1863, President Lincoln declared West Virginia the 35th state, and the capital government moved to Charleston's more central location. Exhibits at Independence Hall illustrate the Union-sympathizing state's secession from the Old Dominion. The courtroom where heated debates occurred has been restored, and visitors can watch a film on those events.

Wheeling is also a center for the arts, as exemplified by Oglebay Institute's **Stifel Fine Arts Center** and the **Wheeling Artisan Center** (wheelingheritage .org). Nor is music neglected: The **Wheeling Jamboree** has featured old and new performers on Saturday nights since 1933. Tickets to the show can be obtained locally or online at wheelingjamboree.org.

Wheeling's Suspension Bridge, built in 1849, still carries traffic to Wheeling Island.

Moundsville to Fairmont

Rippling Farmland & the Palace of Gold

General description: A 57-mile drive through forest, old mining lands, hills, farmland, steep river valleys, and small towns.

Special attractions: Old West Virginia Penitentiary, the ancient Grave Creek Mound Archaeological Complex, the modern Prabhupada's Palace of Gold, covered bridges, Fairmont, and the Mannington Round Barn.

Location: Northern West Virginia.

Driving route numbers: US 250; WV 7.

Travel season: All year.

Camping: None along the drive. Fairmont has a few private campgrounds.

Services: Moundsville and Fairmont have complete services. Gasoline can be found in most small towns along the drive, and a few restaurants operate in the eastern villages.

Nearby attractions: Louis Wetzel Wildlife Management Area, Pricketts Fort State Park, and Valley Falls State Park.

The Route

US 250 could be a time machine, transporting you back to a rural world without fast food, superstores, or even many stoplights. Except for the natural-gas drilling pads dotting the hilltops, you could be traveling in the countryside some 50 years ago. But be careful. For a US highway, US 250 is uncannily like a roller coaster tearing up and down over these rippling hills, and convoys of coal trucks can slow your joy ride.

This time machine, though, has a few time warps, old and new: You'll pass a 2,000-year-old burial mound, a castellated prison from the 1860s, a round dairy barn built in the early 1900s, and the spectacular modern domes and turrets of Prabhupada's Palace of Gold—all within about 40 miles.

The drive begins in the Northern Panhandle in Moundsville on the Ohio River, then heads south and east over the rolling highlands of Mountaineer Country (named for West Virginia University's beloved football team in Morgantown). It ends at Fairmont on the banks of the Monongahela River.

Unearthing the Mystery of the Mound

The drive has an urban but ancient start point. In downtown **Moundsville,** follow the signs to **Grave Creek Mound Archaeological Complex** (wvculture.org), which occupies a sprawling campus at 801 Jefferson St. between 8th and 10th Streets. This 7-acre park surrounds a circular mound, jutting up 69 feet into the cityscape. It is 300 feet in diameter. This mound is the largest of many similar mounds in the eastern US.

Moundsville to Fairmont

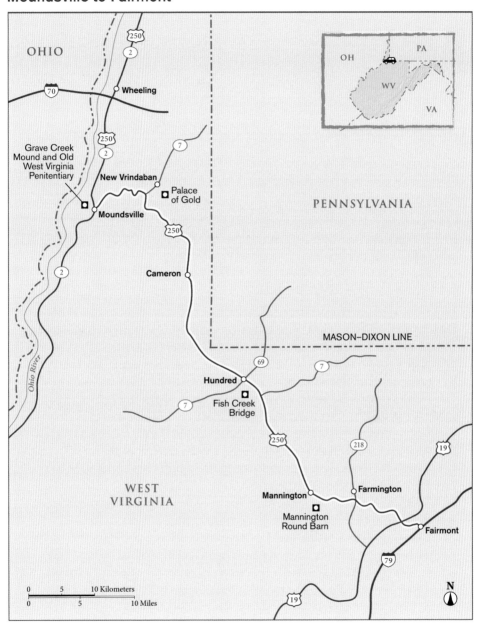

OHIO

250
2

70 — Wheeling

250
2

Grave Creek
Mound and Old
West Virginia
Penitentiary

New Vrindaban

Palace
of Gold

Moundsville

250

2

Cameron

250

7

PENNSYLVANIA

MASON–DIXON LINE

69

7

Hundred

Fish Creek
Bridge

7

WEST
VIRGINIA

250

218

19

Mannington — Farmington

Mannington
Round Barn

Fairmont

79

19

OH — PA

WV

VA

0   5   10 Kilometers
0   5   10 Miles

Ohio River

N

Marshall County near Moundsville dresses up in fall colors.

Early European settlers realized that the mounds were man-made, but they could only speculate as to their age, purpose, and how they were constructed. Some thought they were the remnants of an ancient vanished race of Africans or Europeans; others believed they represented one of the lost tribes of Israel. The people who built these structures were called the Mound Builders by the Europeans.

Excavations in 1838 revealed several human skeletons, plus copper and shell jewelry, and some other artifacts. These included a small flat stone inscribed with unknown characters. This tablet has created much controversy over the years; some say the letters have European or Hebrew origins, but an anthropologist has presented evidence indicating the inscription was a modern forgery.

In 1881 Congress appropriated $5,000 for the Smithsonian Institution to investigate some 2,000 mounds and earthworks in the eastern US. This was the birth of modern American archaeology. These studies indicated that the Mound Builders were not a vanished race but ancestors of the American Indian.

Today the Mound Builders are known as the Adena people, and the mounds, painstakingly built by hand, are considered to be elaborate burial sites for their leaders. The Moundsville mound is believed to have been constructed in stages over a 100-year period from 250 to 150 BC. More than 60,000 tons of soil were carried to the mound, probably in baskets. Originally the mound was surrounded by a 40-foot-wide, 5-foot-deep moat, now mostly filled in.

Visitors enter the park through the adjacent **Delf Norona Museum.** The museum houses a collection of Adena tools, pottery, and other artifacts, as well as exhibits on modern glass, pottery, and other objects of cultural significance.

Colorful exhibits show how the mound was built and how the Adena people lived. Climbing to the top of the mound takes a careful 3-minute walk. The site hosts fossil days, lectures, and even dance concerts. There is a small admission charge for the museum complex.

The top of Grave Creek Mound makes an ideal perch for appreciating the vast size of the former **West Virginia Penitentiary** (wvpentours.com) across the street. The "Pen," as it is known locally, is a massive Gothic-style stone fortress where the state's hardened felons were housed from 1876 to 1995. Even before that, from 1863 to 1865, its original Wagon Gate section held Confederate prisoners. After the war, the prison was enlarged using inmate labor into a small city with its own farm, hospital, carpentry shop, paint shop, stone yard, a brickyard, blacksmith, tailor, and a prison coal mine a mile away. It was virtually self-sufficient.

But despite its castle-like exterior, the Pen was not a pretty place for anyone but the superintendent's family, who lived in nice quarters over the front gate. The 5-by-7-foot cells were cold in the winter and sweltering during the summer. As many as three inmates bunked together in the tiny space. For many years, the facility ranked on the US Department of Justice's list of the top ten most violent correctional facilities. Fights, rapes, and murders were committed in the recreation area.

The prison was declared uninhabitable by the state supreme court and closed down in 1995. For a fee ($8–$15), you can tour the structure, visiting cells, the exercise yard, and "Old Sparky," the electric chair that was in use until 1965 when West Virginia eliminated capital punishment. The penitentiary is open April through November from Tuesday through Sunday for day tours as well as special all-night ghost adventures. Haunted prison tours are available on October nights.

On to the Palace of Gold

After the dark, malevolent atmosphere of the prison, you may be ready to experience a higher vibe. Luckily the rarified halls of the Palace of Gold are only minutes away in the hills above Moundsville. Head east on US 250, which cuts sharply back and forth as it climbs out of the Ohio River Valley. After about 10 miles, just past the small town of Limestone, turn left on WV 7 (Limestone Hill Road) at the sign for New Vrindaban and the **Palace of Gold** (palaceofgold.com).

This narrow road twists and turns past trailers and rural homes as it meanders along the top of an equally narrow ridge for 3 miles. Then, with no warning, the incongruous golden turrets, crenulated domes, and gilded walls of the Palace of Gold spring into sight.

The palace was built as a memorial to Swami Prabhupada, founder of the Krishna Consciousness (Hare Krishna) movement. Prabhupada began his

The Palace of Gold was built by Hare Krishna devotees.

movement in 1965 when he arrived penniless in New York. By 1973, when construction of the Palace of Gold began, he had some 50,000 converts throughout the world. One of 120 temples worldwide and the only one in the US, the Palace of Gold took six years to finish. His followers did the bulk of the work, although most of them had no training in construction. Several dozen Krishna believers live here today.

Tours of the Palace, for which a fee is charged, take visitors over gleaming floors of Italian marble and Iranian onyx, past stained-glass windows adorned with blue peacocks, Lord Krishna's motif, each containing more than 1,500 pieces of hand-cut glass. Crystal chandeliers hang overhead, echoed in the mirrored ceilings and on gold leaf surfaces. Shoe coverings are provided, but you will endear yourself to your tour guide if you remove your footgear and tread gently over the polished floors, continental-Indian style.

The 25-foot central dome features 18 murals depicting the life of Lord Krishna. At the altar a lifelike statue of Prabhupada is seated on a bejeweled golden throne serenely looking over his domain. The tour passes by Prabhupada's apartment, with its bathroom fixtures of solid gold and marble. Hundreds of meticulously hand-painted flowers grace the bedroom ceiling.

Before or after the tour, you are welcome to wander over the grounds and through the gardens, including a prize-winning rose garden. If you get hungry, try the low-cost Palace Restaurant, one of West Virginia's few Indian vegetarian eateries. You might also consider joining residents in meditation at the Sri Sri Radha

Vrindaban Chandra temple. Admission here is free, and the glasswork, ornate altars, and statuary are almost as dazzling as those of the Palace of Gold. The temple is within walking distance of the palace, just beyond the swan pond, which is dominated by huge statues frozen in a worshipful *kirtan* dance. Guest cabins, a guest lodge, and a gift shop are also nearby.

When you leave New Vrindaban, follow WV 7 back to US 250 and turn left. The highway was laid out in the 1930s and takes the high ground over this hilly country. The section covered by this drive now has light traffic, although watch out for coal trucks. It's not relaxing being enveloped in a convoy of these gear-grinding behemoths.

As you enter the small town of **Cameron,** a few brick buildings stand marooned on the hillside; the rest of the small town is clustered below. Actually, the 2- and 3-story Classical Revival buildings hearken back to a time before an 1895 fire burned the heart out of downtown Cameron, destroying 58 buildings and prompting a law forbidding new downtown buildings constructed of wood. The historic buildings left include a flatiron building and the skinny, brick B&O Freight Station that curves along the curving railroad track.

Cameron's fire history instigated its other claim to fame, its historic semi-circular swimming pool. One of the New Deal's Public Works Administration (WPA) projects in 1939, the pool was viewed as a potential water supply in emergency situations. The pool was built with an imported sandy beach skirting its sides, colored floodlights for night swimming, and an underwater lifeguard room with portholes for viewing the pool bottom. Still in operation, the pool is considered the last remaining example of a WPA pool with these modern features.

Crossing the Mason-Dixon Line

A few miles beyond Cameron, you leave Marshall County and enter Wetzel County. The east–west county line marks the **Mason-Dixon Line,** the traditional boundary between the South and North. Properly known as Mason and Dixon's Line, it was surveyed by English astronomers Charles Mason and Jeremiah Dixon from 1763 to 1767 to settle a boundary dispute between colonies. At latitude 39° 43' 19.11", it later came to symbolize the boundary between free and slave states. Today it marks much of the southern border of Pennsylvania with both Maryland and West Virginia

A few miles below the Mason-Dixon Line lies the little town of **Hundred,** named for Henry Church, a longtime resident. As a young man Church was a soldier in the British army. During the Battle of Yorktown, Virginia, in 1781, he was captured by American troops. After the conflict he settled here; over the years he was recognized as the local patriarch. When his age extended beyond the century mark, he became known as "Old Hundred." After his death in 1869 at the age of 109, the settlement became known as Hundred.

As you leave Hundred, on the right you will spot Rush Run Road (CR 13) and the **Fish Creek Covered Bridge.** Constructed in 1881 and still in use, the Fish Creek Bridge is a 36-foot-long kingpost truss span.

In the 1800s designers, craftsmen, and builders considered their covered bridges both functional and beautiful. The delicate wooden support arches and trusses were well protected by the walls and roof. With the coming of the railroads and their easily constructed and more durable steel bridges, wooden covered bridges became less important. Many fell into disrepair. By the 1930s about 100 covered bridges were still standing in West Virginia, but only 17 survive today. The ones that remain are again highly valued, but more for their beauty, workmanship, heritage, and history than for their role as arteries of transportation.

Covered bridges are not the only roadside remnants of the early 1900s. Look for several old barns with faded painted sides that urge you to chew Mail Pouch Tobacco. During the hard times of the Great Depression, farmers with barns visible from the road were happy to receive a free barn painting from tobacco companies. It made little difference if the side facing the highway was an advertisement.

The drive follows several small streams and crosses Buffalo Creek in **Mannington.** In downtown Mannington the West Augusta Historical Society maintains a small museum of historical artifacts in an old schoolhouse. An early 1912 caboose and an 1870 log cabin share the historical society's grounds.

The Mannington Round Barn

A few blocks past the museum, turn right on Flaggy Meadow Road and follow the signs to the **Mannington Round Barn,** also maintained by the West Augusta Historical Society. Built in 1912, this is the only round barn in the state and is listed on the National Register of Historical Places.

This dairy barn was built by farmer Amos C. Hamilton. Farmers liked round barns because the large loft on the top floor gave them lots of storage space for hay. In addition to hay, this 3-story barn housed cows on the ground floor and the Hamilton family on the second. Today it is filled with Hamilton mementos and old farm equipment such as butter churns, a horse-drawn potato picker, and a child's sled. You'll also see the Hamiltons' living quarters and the spring-fed automatic watering system for cows. Several flights of narrow stairs lead up to the cupola for an interesting view of the neighborhood.

A nominal donation is requested for both the museum and the round barn. Both buildings are open on Sunday afternoon between Memorial Day and Labor

The Mannington Round Barn once housed a family as well as farm implements.

Day or at other times by appointment. See the appendix for the phone number and address.

Mannington grew rapidly after petroleum was discovered here in 1869. The original well was one of the first drilled on geological evidence; its location was based on the then-new "anticlinal theory," the discovery that oil was found under folded arches—anticlines—and domes of subsurface rock. Later, coal mining provided jobs for many workers.

Five miles east is the village of **Farmington.** In 1968, a fiery explosion ripped through Farmington's No. 9 Mine, killing 78 miners. The bodies of 19 of those men were never recovered, so the mine shaft was sealed off as a tomb. A memorial stands near the entrance, about a mile north of Farmington on WV 218. Each November, surviving miners, families, and others hold a memorial in the hollow where the monument is located. As a result of the Farmington disaster, Congress passed the 1969 Coal Mine Safety and Health Act, increasing mine inspections and bolstering safety standards.

From Farmington it is about 7 miles on US 250 to Fairmont and the end of the drive. In nearby **Barrackville** is the 146-foot-long Barrackville Covered Bridge—almost three times as long as the Fish Creek Covered Bridge. In Fairmont, be sure to drive by High Gate, a coal baron's Tudor Revival mansion on Fairmont Avenue between 8th and 9th Streets. The first Father's Day observance in the US was held in 1908 here on Fairmont Avenue at Central United Methodist Church. The preceding December, a mine explosion in nearby Monongah had killed 362 men, leaving more than 1,000 children grieving. Grace Fletcher Clayton, a minister's daughter, persuaded her pastor to perform a special mass to remember and honor fathers. Although Father's Day didn't become an annual event for 64 years, the Fairmont event was significant for the hundreds who attended. A historical marker on the right side of Fairmont Avenue marks the location. On down the street, you can't miss the pink-and-aqua Poky Dot restaurant, which has been serving the food of the 1950s for more than 50 years.

Another significant sight is the Robert Mollohan-Jefferson Street Bridge, known as the Million Dollar Bridge, over the Monongahela. The arched structure was built in 1921 and restored in 2000. The town is home to Fairmont State College, established in 1867. The campus maintains the Snodgrass School, a 23-by-26-foot one-room schoolhouse, originally built in 1871. Hikers and cyclists might want to check out the 16-mile **West Fork River Rail Trail** (mcparc.com), which runs from Fairmont south to Shinnston through several old coal towns.

North of town is **Pricketts Fort State Park** (prickettsfortstatepark.com), restored to look as it did in 1774, where costumed interpreters demonstrate what life was like in frontier colonial days. South of town, the Tygart River flows through a narrow canyon at **Valley Falls State Park** (valleyfallsstatepark.com). Hiking, picnicking, and mountain biking are popular at this day-use facility.

3

Along the Ohio River

New Martinsville to Parkersburg

General description: A 50-mile drive on a paved, two-lane highway along the Ohio River past scenic islands and historical oil and gas boomtowns. The area is mostly rural but with some industrial development.

Special attractions: Bluffs of the Ohio River, Hannibal Locks and Dam, Ohio River Islands National Wildlife Refuge, historic Sistersville and its antique operating oil well, Sistersville Ferry, Parkersburg, and Blennerhassett Island Historical State Park.

Location: Western West Virginia, along the Ohio River.

Driving route numbers: WV 2, 31.

Travel season: All year. Blennerhassett Island and several other attractions are closed during the colder months.

Camping: The closest public campground is at North Bend State Park, about 20 miles east of Parkersburg on US 50, with 77 sites and all facilities. Two private campgrounds are near Parkersburg.

Services: All services are available in most towns.

Nearby attractions: Wayne National Forest (in Ohio, across the river), Blennerhassett Island Historic State Park, and North Bend State Park and Rail Trail.

The Route

For about 250 miles the Ohio River marks the border of West Virginia and Ohio. Scenic Route 1, Northern Panhandle, describes scenes along the panhandle and northern section of the Ohio River from Chester, at the northern tip of West Virginia, to Wheeling.

This drive begins on the Ohio River at New Martinsville, 45 miles south of Wheeling, and follows WV 2 along the river 50 miles south to Parkersburg. Wayne National Forest borders the river on the Ohio side for much of the drive, and 11 islands are a part of the Ohio River Islands National Wildlife Refuge. Much of this stretch is thinly settled and relatively undeveloped.

At **New Martinsville** the river flows along a flat valley with rocky bluffs 150 feet high on the West Virginia side. The 250-year-old town, once known as Martin's Fort, was named for Presley Martin, leader of the fort and small community. As the country prospered in the early 1800s, the Ohio River became an important highway for trade and travel between Fort Pitt (Pittsburgh) and New Orleans, and Martin's Fort flourished as an important port of call along the river.

The shape of river travel has changed, and today coal-hauling barges and iron freighters have replaced side-wheelers and wooden flatboats. This traffic has been made possible by construction of 53 dams and sets of locks along the 981 river-miles of the Ohio River from Pittsburgh to Cairo, Illinois, where the Ohio joins

Along the Ohio River

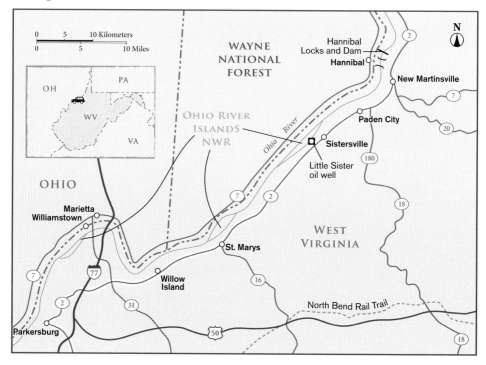

the Mississippi. The dams, built and operated by the US Army Corps of Engineers, provide pools of water deep enough for year-round navigation, and the locks raise or lower the boats to gently accommodate the 460-foot difference in elevation between Pittsburgh and Cairo.

The 1,089-foot-long **Hannibal Locks and Dam** (lrp.usace.army.mil/nav/hanni.htm) dominates the river in New Martinsville. Although security measures now keep visitors a good distance from the locks, a small park on the Ohio side of the river displays historic locks and gives a view of lock operations through a chain-link fence. From WV 2 at the northern end of New Martinsville, cross over the river on the high arch of the Korean War Veteran's Memorial Bridge. Passengers will have excellent views of the dam, river, town, and surrounding countryside. The parking area for the dam is to the right as you leave the bridge in Hannibal, Ohio.

Locks here raise or lower vessels 21 feet. The main lock, 1,200 feet long, can accommodate the longest coal barge on the river. The facility averages 350 lockages a month—more than 11 per day—so your chances of seeing a vessel pass through a lock are good.

Exhibits on the grounds of the visitor center include the remains of a historic wicket dam and a maneuver boat, used for driving pilings in the river. Other exhibits depict the history of navigation on the Ohio River and have information about the US Army Corps of Engineers.

Drive back over the bridge and turn right (south) on WV 2 through New Martinsville. The town is a center for river-based recreation, with a county-maintained fishing pier and marina. The historical area features several 1890s Victorian buildings, the most notable of which is the multiturreted Wetzel County Courthouse.

Glassmaking was once a major industry along the Ohio River Valley, and several local factories used to offer tours of their operations. The plants in New Martinsville and nearby Paden City have closed, except for Marble King, which no longer offers tours.

You travel south on WV 2 from New Martinsville as the Ohio River Valley widens several miles, often bordered by cliffs 200 to 300 feet high. Side streams enter the valley through broad, steep gullies.

Ohio River Islands National Wildlife Refuge

South of Paden City, you may begin to notice islands in the Ohio River. Teen-age surveyor George Washington noticed them, too, and reported the Ohio River being "crowded with islands." Today 22 of these islands along the 362 miles of river from Pennsylvania to Kentucky form the **Ohio River Islands National Wildlife Refuge.** Their natural beauty is enhanced by the Wayne National Forest, which borders the Ohio side of the river from just north of Paden City to a few miles north of Parkersburg.

As northern continental glaciers melted near the end of the Pleistocene epoch, a surging current of meltwater flowed down the Ohio River, carrying enormous amounts of gravel, sand, silt, and other debris. After the ice melted, the flow decreased, and much of the debris was deposited in the river as the numerous islands.

The refuge and islands protect some of the last remnants of habitat along the river for shorebirds, waterfowl, songbirds, freshwater fish, and mussels. More than 160 species of birds are found in the refuge, including great blue herons in rookeries. The shallow back channels are important nursery and feeding areas for some of the 50 species of warm-water fish. Beaver, mink, muskrat, cottontail rabbit, opossum, raccoon, and white-tailed deer are common island mammals. Yes, deer do swim the river.

Hundreds of years before Europeans came to the area, the islands were well known to the Indians, according to archeological evidence found on several islands. When George Washington surveyed the Ohio, 57 islands graced the river;

41 remain today. The rest were carried away on barges as gravel and sand. Most of the river, including the islands, lies within West Virginia.

Eleven of the refuge islands are clustered in a 20-mile stretch of river between New Martinsville and St. Marys along this drive. Most of them are accessible only by boat, but at St. Marys, almost 30 miles south of New Martinsville, a short bridge gives you the opportunity to visit Middle Island, one of the most accessible and beautiful islands in the refuge. This quiet island is a prime spot for fishing and viewing waterfowl. Turn right on George Street to reach the bridge.

A few miles past Paden City, you come to the quiet little town of **Sistersville.** In the 1880s the 500 residents made their living in agriculture or servicing the river trade.

This era ended virtually overnight in 1889, when oil was discovered in the area. Thirty years earlier oil and gas had propelled Parkersburg into boomtown status, and the possibility of similar fortunes in Sistersville ignited the hopes and dreams of many. Geologists, speculators, bankers, businessmen, fortune seekers, and camp followers poured into the area, eager to get their share of the wealth from black gold. Soon oil derricks covered the hills and many backyards, and the clanking of pumps and the smell of crude oil permeated the atmosphere.

As the oil began to flow, so did the money. More than 100 oil companies located here, and the population grew to over 15,000. The new wealth prompted a flurry of construction, resulting in ornate Victorian mansions and company buildings. The now-affluent community built modern public schools, a city-operated hospital, a municipal electric-power station, and a trolley line to surrounding towns. The boom also drew in breweries, saloons, brothels, casinos, hotels, and theaters, including an opera house offering first-run shows and vaudeville acts from New York.

By 1915 the oil was played out. Most people lost their jobs or abandoned their businesses and left—some penniless, some with fortunes. Within a few years the wells and derricks disappeared. The townspeople who remained had mostly prospered from the boom. A large district of fashionable homes and buildings remained.

Today the town, with its well-maintained century-old buildings, is listed as a National Historic District. You can obtain a free map of the historical district at the distinctive diamond-shaped city hall, which straddles the intersection of Main and Diamond. This historical structure was built in 1897 in the American colonial style. Nearby is the 1895 Wells Inn, harboring a pool in its basement.

Looking back at the town of St. Mary's from St. Mary's Island in the Ohio.

Still Pumping: The Little Sister Oil Well

A few blocks from the Wells Inn, the restored **Little Sister oil well** and derrick towers along the Ohio shoreline, one of the last remnants of the hundreds of wells that once covered the landscape. No mere decoration, this well is operational. Each September it pumps up some souvenir black gold during the West Virginia Oil & Gas Festival.

Adjacent to the well is the terminal for the Sistersville Ferry, really a barge and a tug, which has been crossing to Fly, Ohio, at this spot since 1817. The Sistersville Ferry is the only ferry operating on the Ohio in West Virginia, and it transports nearly 100 cars across the river each day mid-April through early November. Without the 15-minute ferry commute, many people would have to loop south to St. Marys Bridge, 20 minutes away. The town-owned ferry charges a small fee to motorists and pedestrians.

Back on the drive, continue south on WV 2, passing several Victorian mansions as you leave town. The river widens, and the countryside becomes more open with lower, gentler hills. Several working oil and gas wells indicate that the petroleum industry still has some role in the economy. There is little new drilling for oil, although natural gas drilling is moving into the area.

From St. Marys continue south on WV 2. Manufacturing plants and other businesses begin to dominate the scenery. As you approach the town of Willow Island, you'll see the huge cooling towers of Willow Run Nuclear Plant issuing plumes of steam. In Waverly, WV 2 leaves the river and continues straight about 5 miles to the southern end of the drive in Parkersburg. For a tasty detour, turn right on WV14 in North Parkersburg, then swing left on the first block of River Road to the renowned **Holl's Chocolates** confectionary where you can see and sample chocolates made the old Swiss way.

Parkersburg, where the Little Kanawha River flows into the Ohio, became the first oil-industry boomtown in the US back in 1859. The **Oil and Gas Museum** (oilandgasmuseum.com) tells this fascinating story and contains extensive exhibits of drilling equipment and paraphernalia. The yard is dense with larger pieces of equipment, such as a 1905 steam engine and a nodding-donkey-style pump. A panoramic geologic map shows the location of more than 10,000 wells drilled in the state since 1859. The town's Julia-Ann Square Historical District, a collection of 126 strikingly elegant homes, makes a nice walking tour, especially around the time of the Easter parade or the district's Victorian garden tour. This town has other riches, including its 1889 Blennerhassett Hotel, Smoot Theatre, and the Blennerhassett Museum downtown. **Blennerhassett Island Historical State Park** (blennerhassettislandstatepark.com), with its reconstructed 7,000-square-foot Blennerhassett Mansion, sits on an island in the Ohio, a

Blennerhassett Mansion is accessible only by a 20-minute stern-wheeler voyage.

20-minute stern-wheeler ride away from town. Visitors can purchase tickets at the Blennerhassett Museum for a boat ride to the island during the state park's open season, May through October. Originally built in 1801, the exquisitely furnished mansion was the site of intrigue. The owner, Harman Blennerhassett, apparently plotted with statesman Aaron Burr there to establish a new country in the Spanish territory in the Southwest. The plot was discovered, and both men arrested. Although they were eventually acquitted, the Blennerhassetts were ruined financially and politically.

4

Kingwood to Cathedral State Park

Through the Cheat River Gorge

General description: This 26-mile drive follows the gorge of the Cheat River and then visits the virgin hemlocks and hardwoods of Cathedral State Park.

Special attractions: Cheat River gorge and Cathedral State Park.

Location: Northwestern West Virginia.

Driving route numbers: US 50; WV 7, 72.

Travel season: All year. For an unforgettable experience visit Cathedral State Park during peak fall colors or after a winter snowstorm.

Camping: None along the drive. At Albright, north of Kingwood, is a small private campground.

Services: All services are available along the drive.

Nearby attractions: Arthurdale New Deal Historic District, Fairfax Stone, Monongahela National Forest, and Our Lady of the Pines shrine in Silver Lake.

The Route

From Kingwood this 26-mile drive mostly follows the gorge of the Cheat River and ends at a majestic virgin forest at Cathedral State Park. The entire drive is over hard-surfaced, all-weather roads.

Kingwood sits on a high bluff above the Cheat River. The former mining town has a young spirit and is known now as the jumping-off spot for raft trips down the raging Cheat. Coal mines still operate, but at a fraction of the tonnage of their peak years, and the town's economy is as much tied to the nearby US Army National Guard base as to coal.

The railroads have suffered, too. Kingwood and the state lost a treasured icon when the West Virginia Northern (WVN) Railroad made its last run in November 1999, a few months after the railroad's 100th birthday.

The WVN began in 1899 as a narrow-gauge line hauling coal from local mines. At the height of coal mining activity during World War II, the WVN was loading coal from 19 mines along its 11-mile route from Kingwood to Tunnelton. On most days a 50-car train hauled coal along the route, but on peak days 200 cars were required. At Tunnelton the coal cars were switched to the main line of the Baltimore & Ohio Railroad.

As some mines closed and others began hauling coal by truck, the WVN was forced to cease activity in 1991. A local corporation was chartered to operate the

Kingwood to Cathedral State Park

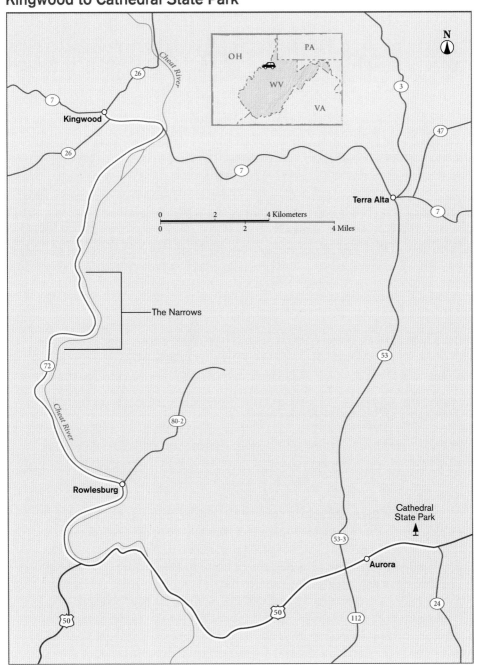

The highway borders Cheat River's whitewater rapids for several miles.
WEST VIRGINIA DEPARTMENT OF COMMERCE, STEPHEN SHALUTA

line as a passenger excursion train until late 1999 when it, too, was forced to close for financial reasons. The nonprofit Friends of the Cheat is now working to create a Kingwood–Tunnelton rail trail that will run 10 miles over the old railroad line.

Through the Cheat River Valley

From Kingwood go south on WV 72, which follows the Cheat River. Across the river you'll see the 5,000-foot runway of Camp Dawson, a US Army airfield and training center. Soon the river valley closes in, and steep hills rise from either bank.

The **Cheat River,** along with the New and Gauley, make up the "Big Three" of West Virginia's whitewater rafting rivers. This section of the Cheat, known as the Narrows, borders WV 72 for several miles and is one of the few places where motorists can drive for any distance along a major whitewater river. Considered suitable for beginning rafters and families, the rapids in the Narrows are rated from II to IV. (I is very mild; VI is virtually unrunnable for most paddlers.)

The Cheat can be run year-round, but it is most popular in late spring when snowmelt from mountains to the south brings the highest water levels. The wildest section of the Cheat, the Canyon, begins north of Kingwood and runs through remote, roadless country to Cheat Lake and its dam, near Morgantown. For experts only, the Canyon has miles of nonstop rapids that are rated from III to V, or even VI when the water is highest.

Rafters may or may not be running the Cheat, depending on the weather and water level. You will see a few coal mines and a cement plant across the river, as well as the town of Rowlesburg, spread out along the narrow valley.

At the stop sign and intersection with US 50, turn east (left). US 50, also known as the Northwestern Turnpike, was surveyed in the early 1800s by the French engineer Claude Crozet. Following game trails and Indian paths, he laid out a route from the Shenandoah Valley of Virginia to the Ohio River. Before the days of interstates, US 50 was a main east–west highway, a ribbon of road across the continent from the Atlantic shores of Maryland to the California coast. (It now ends at Sacramento.) The highway has a mystique second only to that of old US 66.

US 50 follows the gorge of the Cheat River, here reduced to minor rapids, for a few miles and then begins a long climb out of the deep valley onto a rolling plateau. Outside Aurora, you will begin to see a thick forest of huge majestic trees. This is **Cathedral State Park** (cathedralstatepark.com), 133 acres of the last stand of virgin mixed timber in the state.

500-Year-Old Trees

A rare eastern forest of virgin hemlocks up to 12 stories high and 20 feet in circumference—a few are 500 years old—this West Virginia state park is designated a Natural Historical Landmark. It's good you're visiting now. The awe-inspiring hemlocks may not always be here.

The forest is under death threat from the woolly adelgid, a tiny insect that sucks the life from hemlock needles. As average temperatures climb, populations of hemlock woolly adelgids are creeping up the mountains and farther north. Named for its wool-like filament, hemlock woolly adelgid first appeared on the East Coast in the early 1950s and quickly became established in the dense forests of Virginia. Adelgid infestations can kill a hemlock in just a few years, sucking it dry of essential nutrients. With two generations produced each year, adelgids can quickly spread to new territory. They have been spotted in Cathedral State Park, although they haven't yet altered the humid, magical ambience of woodland shaded by a canopy of hemlocks.

Biologists have been experimenting with a natural predator of the adelgid, a black lady beetle they brought in from Japan. The beetles are doing their job. Each larva consumes up to 200 adelgid eggs.

Other large trees—red oak, maple, beech, black cherry, and yellow birch—accompany the hemlocks, like the supporting instruments to a master virtuoso.

Several miles of trails thread through the woods, shaded on even the sunniest of days by the green needles of the hemlocks far overhead.

At one time much of West Virginia looked like this. Because it was part of an old resort, these woods were saved from the lumberman's ax at a time when the state was virtually clear-cut. Later the property was deeded to the state. The park is open 365 days a year. Tours can be arranged by advance reservation.

The drive ends here. Five miles south of the park via WV 24 in Silver Lake is Our Lady of the Pines chapel. Measuring just 24 by 12 feet, with barely enough room inside for 12 worshippers, it is said to be the smallest church in the lower 48 states.

Cathedral State Park's 400-year-old hemlocks are the state's last virgin stand.

5

Romney–Keyser Loop

Route of the Potomac Eagle

General description: A 55-mile loop drive from Romney, home of the Potomac Eagle Scenic Railroad, to Keyser, through low hills and farmland and along the South Branch of the Potomac River.

Special attractions: Potomac Eagle Scenic Railroad, oldest Confederate monument, Indian Mound Cemetery, Fort Mill Ridge Civil War trenches, Fort Ashby, and views of the South Branch of the Potomac.

Location: Northeastern West Virginia.

Driving route numbers: US 50, 220; WV 28, 46.

Travel season: All year. The Potomac Eagle runs during warmer months only. Fall foliage trips may require advance reservations.

Camping: Near Romney are several private campgrounds.

Services: All services are available along the drive.

Nearby attractions: Nancy Hanks Memorial and Waffle Rock at Jennings Randolph Lake.

The Route

This 55-mile drive begins at historic Romney, heads west on US 50 and then north on US 220 to Keyser, then loops back via WV 46 and WV 28 past restored Fort Ashby and along the South Branch of the Potomac River back to Romney. Most of the drive is through farm- and pastureland, with some forested areas. It also passes through small gaps in the low-lying mountains. The complete drive can be made in about 2 hours.

If your primary focus is the Potomac Eagle Scenic Railroad and you have limited time, an alternative to the complete loop is the especially scenic drive north of Romney on WV 28 along South Branch Valley.

US 50 started as an Indian trail, and Romney, one of the oldest towns in the state, was incorporated in 1762. The town saw lots of action during the Civil War as it seesawed from one side to the other more than 50 times. The effects of the Civil War are still imprinted on this little town, in the well-preserved Civil War battle trenches at Fort Mill Ridge Wildlife Management Area and in the numerous graves at Indian Mound Cemetery (historichampshire.org) beside US 50 on the right as you leave town.

In fact, **Romney** (historichampshire.org) lays claim to having the first Confederate monument to be erected. In the years immediately after the Civil War, federal law forbade monuments honoring the Confederate States of America. But a large group of Hampshire ladies raised funds for a white Italian marble statue bearing the inscription "The Daughters of Old Hampshire erect this tribute of affection to her heroic Sons, who fell in defense of Southern Rights." The last

Romney-Keyser Loop

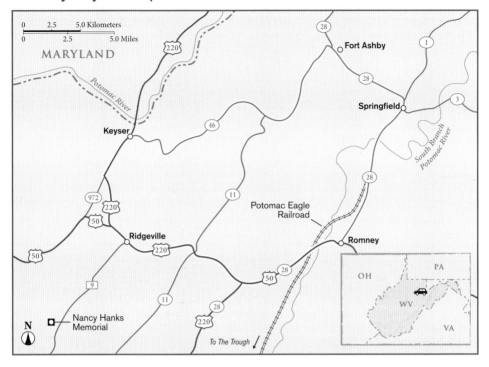

two words probably made the monument illegal, so "Southern Rights" was not added until the statue was boxed for shipment. The Baltimore stone carver added "Southern Rights" through a small opening in the packaging, and the monument was dedicated at Indian Mound Cemetery on September 26, 1867.

Most people, however, come to town for the train. It's an almost guaranteed way to see eagles—the **Potomac Eagle Scenic Railroad** (potomaceagle.info) on the outskirts of Romney. This excursion train offers a 3-hour trip along the South Branch of the Potomac. The highlight of the tour is **The Trough,** a narrow, steep-walled, 17-mile-long gorge that is one of the few nesting places in the state for the American bald eagle. Eagles are spotted on 9 out of 10 train trips. You'll see these majestic birds soaring through the gorge on thermals, and you may be lucky enough to see one of them swoop down to the river and snag a tasty fish. You can't drive through The Trough; the only way to get there is by train or canoe.

In addition to eagles you'll see hawks, deer, and maybe beaver. Look for bass in the clear waters below as the train crosses the river on trestles. You can ride in an enclosed coach, but photographers may prefer the open gondola car. For the ultimate in comfort, pay a little more for the club car.

The train runs several times a day during the warmer months. Reservations are recommended in October when the fall foliage lights up the gorge in neon yellow and orange. Special excursion trips are featured May through November.

The automobile part of this scenic drive starts in Romney and goes west on US 50. As you cross the South Branch of the Potomac, you also cross the tracks of the Potomac Eagle. Just after this look for the small sign on your left for the **Fort Mill Ridge Wildlife Management Area** (wvdnr.gov/hunting). If you're a Civil War buff, the battle trenches still visible at the edge of the forest will give you chills. The trenches were dug and lined with chestnut logs by the Confederate artillery in 1861–1862 and taken over by the Yankees in 1863. Back on US 50, leave the Potomac River valley through a small gap and bear right on US 50/220 at the village of Junction. The hills become somewhat larger as you proceed west. At Ridgeville at the foot of Knobly Mountain, a side trip on CR 9 (becoming CR 3 at the county line) leads south (left) to the **birthplace of Nancy Hanks,** mother of President Abraham Lincoln.

After the gap through Knobly Mountain, go north (right) on US 220 where it splits from US 50. Ahead you'll see the long ridge of Fore Knobs, which forms the imposing Allegheny Front to the southwest.

This takes you into **Keyser,** the county seat of Mineral County. The campus of Potomac State College, a center for the performing arts, adorns the hillside on the left. On the other side of town, turn east (right) on WV 46. This less-traveled road passes farms and woods to Fort Ashby.

The palisaded wooden logs of **Fort Ashby** look much as they did in 1755, one of 69 forts young army officer George Washington ordered built to protect this area during the French and Indian Wars. In fact, Fort Ashby is considered the only fort from the French and Indian War still intact and supported by its original timbers. It was originally a log stockade with four corner blockhouses and log barracks, but the single log cabin is all that remains after more than 250 years. The only major battle at Fort Ashby occurred when Lieutenant Robert Rutherford and his rangers were ambushed outside the fort by a band of Indians. During the siege, Colonel John Ashby made a remarkable escape to the fort that eventually took his name. Fort Ashby probably owes its survival to the fact that families used it as a home from the 1760s until 1927. The last owner was about to tear it down when the Daughters of the American Revolution (DAR) at Keyser bought it. The Works Progress Administration restored it in the 1930s, and it is now owned and operated by the Fort Ashby Chapter DAR, who give tours on special occasions and by request (see appendix).

Back on the drive, turn right on WV 28 in the village of Fort Ashby. Past Springfield, the drive parallels the South Fork of the Potomac, a winding, lazy river at this point and a popular recreation area for fishing, boating, and swimming. The drive follows the river past the station for the Potomac Eagle to Romney and the end of the drive.

The Potomac Eagle travels through the remote Trough, where eagles are frequently sighted. West Virginia Department of Commerce, Stephen Shaluta

6

Berkeley Springs to Paw Paw

Springs, Spas & Tunnels

General description: A 30-mile drive from the baths of Berkeley Springs past the Panorama Overlook along Cacapon River to the Paw Paw Tunnel at the Chesapeake & Ohio National Historic Canal.

Special attractions: The spas, baths, shops, and sights of Berkeley Springs; Panorama Overlook; Cacapon Mountain and Cacapon River; and the Paw Paw Tunnel of the Chesapeake & Ohio Historic Canal at the Potomac River.

Location: Eastern West Virginia.

Driving route numbers: WV 9; MD 51.

Travel season: All year.

Camping: Primitive campsites are at the end of the drive at the C&O Canal at Paw Paw.

Services: All services are available in Berkeley Springs at the start of the drive, but little is available along the route.

Nearby attractions: Cacapon Resort State Park, Martinsburg (see Scenic Route 7).

The Route

If there is a theme for this 30-mile drive, it is "water." Start with ablutions at the bubbling town of **Berkeley Springs** (berkeleysprings.com), famed since colonial days for its warm mineralized baths. Then head west across Cacapon Ridge with its outstanding views of the Potomac River. Follow sinuous Cacapon River through thick woods to the town of Paw Paw. The drive ends on the Maryland side of the Potomac River at the Chesapeake & Ohio Canal National Historic Park, where you can hike along the canal towpath and through the 3,118-foot-long Paw Paw Tunnel. This relatively short drive can be combined with Scenic Route 7, which travels from Harpers Ferry to Berkeley Springs.

The first bathers at Berkeley Springs were members of various Indian tribes who refreshed themselves in the warm water that gurgled out of the limestone rock. Teenage George Washington first visited the springs on a surveying trip in 1748; over the next 50 years he frequently brought his family here to drink and bathe in the lightly mineralized water.

In 1776 Washington bought two lots and named the town Bath, still the official name for the town, after the ancient spa of the same name in England. Other members of the Washington family also owned land in the area. After he became president, Washington spent several weeks each summer here, establishing what some have called the "first Summer White House."

Berkeley Springs to Paw Paw

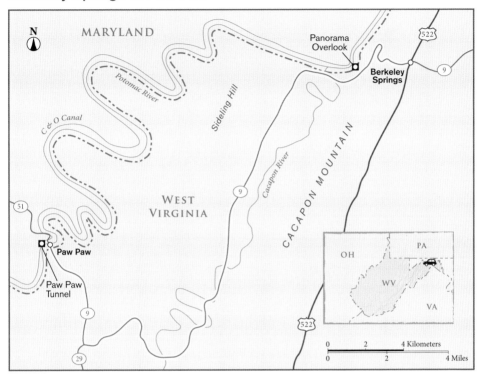

George Washington's Bathtub

Today **Berkeley Springs State Park** (wvstateparks.com/park/berkeley-springs-state-park) sits in the center of town. Visitors can fill their jugs at the spring's public tap and swim in the adjacent pool in summer. Tucked into the side of the park is George Washington's Bathtub, where the teenage surveyor reputedly washed away the grime and tiredness after a hard day's work.

The square is flanked by two public bathhouses. The Roman Bath House, built in 1815, features 9 private bathing rooms, each with a 5-by-9-foot chamber large enough to pack in four very close friends, but cozy for two. The tubs are available by the half hour. Upstairs is a small museum telling the story of Berkeley Springs and its water.

Across the square is the more luxurious Main Bath House, where you can combine a soaking with a steam bath or massage. Water bubbles from the ground at the rate of 2,000 gallons per minute at a temperature of 74 degrees, perhaps warm enough for George, but a tad cool for a relaxing soak. It's heated today to a soporific 100–102 degrees, or cooler if you request.

Folks have been coming to soak in Berkeley Springs' warm mineral waters for at least 270 years.

Prices at the state bathhouses are reasonable, less than $100 for a 1-hour combination massage and soak, and a little more than half that for a simple bath and shower. Advance reservations are recommended, particularly on weekends and holidays. If the state park's public baths can't accommodate you, there are numerous private spas and bathhouses in town that can. Many are more luxurious than the state facilities and offer additional amenities, including mud wraps, manicures, traditional massages, and a variety of exotic massages such as the Thai technique. The local phone book lists more massage therapists than lawyers, which some residents consider a sign of the town's enlightenment.

When you've had enough water, you can visit Berkeley Springs's numerous art galleries, crafts and specialty shops, antiques stores, and small restaurants. Only a 3-hour drive from Washington, D. C., the area is attracting many weekend visitors who, like the first president, come here to relax and escape the big city.

One of the unique events this historic spa town offers is the annual **Berkeley Springs International Water Tasting.** Judges sip goblets of spring water, mineral water, sparkling water, even tap water submitted from around the world. In a blind judging, these waters are graded for flavor, odor, aftertaste, and smoothness or harshness in the mouth. The winners may be surprising; cities like Atlantic City, New Jersey, and Lansing, Michigan, have beat out more exotic locales in the municipal tap-water category. Other recent winners have hailed from New Zealand, Macedonia, and Canada. Held the last weekend in February, this is the finale of the winter Festival of Water.

When you're ready to tear yourself away from Berkeley Springs, begin the scenic drive by heading west from the center of town on WV 9. As the drive ascends Warm Springs Ridge, a spur of Cacapon Mountain, you pass the **Berkeley Castle,** which overlooks the town like a sentinel. This replica of an English Norman castle was built in 1885 as a man's wedding gift to his younger wife. Although he didn't live to see the six-year project to completion, his wife had the castle finished according to his plans. The castle has been saved from destruction and renovated several times, and it is available for weddings and private events but not for tours.

The rock beneath Warm Springs Ridge is the Oriskany sandstone. This rock is an ancient beach deposit of pure quartz sand—silica—that was laid down at the edge of the ancestral North American continent during the Devonian period. Because of its purity, the Oriskany sandstone is in demand for glassmaking, stoneware, and other operations that require high-grade silica. About 40 quarries in the state extract less-pure sandstone to use as a construction aggregate, but the only major glass sand company in West Virginia lies about 5 miles south along Warm Springs Ridge. This quarry opened during the Civil War and still produces tons of high-grade silica each year.

The Panorama Overlook

The drive zigzags upward, and after 3 miles, reaches the **Panorama Overlook** just below the 1,000-foot summit of Prospect Peak, the northern end of long Cacapon Mountain. From this spot you can see West Virginia on the near side of the Potomac River, Maryland farmland on the far side, and the hazy blue mountains of Pennsylvania in the distance. The jagged mountains to the left mark the beginning of the Eastern Continental Divide. The Museum of Natural History in New York rates Panorama's view the fifth finest in the US, while *National Geographic* calls it the "Switzerland View of America."

The road winds down the mountain to the village of Great Cacapon along the banks of the Potomac River at the confluence of the Cacapon River. Continuing west and south on WV 9, the towns grow smaller and the hills grow larger as the drive follows the Cacapon River Valley upstream along the long ridge of Cacapon Mountain. The drive is lined with thick hardwoods and pines between crossings of the sinuous Cacapon River.

At the intersection with WV 29, bear right (northwest), following WV 9 to the town of **Paw Paw** on the Potomac River. This was an important staging area during the Civil War for Union troops, when as many as 16,000 federal soldiers camped in the vicinity. The town (and tunnel, which you will reach in a few

West Virginia bananas, otherwise known as pawpaws, grow along the Potomac River.

minutes) are named after the pawpaw tree, *Asimina triloba,* which grows in abundance in the area. An American native related to the mango, the large, sweet pawpaw fruit ripens in September. Its fragrance permeates the area, making it difficult to beat out the raccoons for a taste of this wild fruit known as the West Virginia banana. But it is well worth trying.

The Chesapeake & Ohio Canal National Historic Park

Follow WV 9 through town across the Potomac River into Maryland, where the route number changes to MD 51. The drive ends in a quarter mile at the picnic and camping area of the **Chesapeake & Ohio Canal National Historic Park** (nps .gov/choh) on the banks of the Potomac River.

The C&O Canal follows the Maryland shore of the Potomac River for 184 miles from Georgetown in Washington, D.C., to Cumberland, Maryland. It was built with picks and shovels over a 22-year period beginning in 1828. The tunnel is 3,118 feet long, and you can barely see a light at the other end when you step into the entrance. The Paw Paw Tunnel was built to bypass 6 miles of looping shoreline and cliffs at the Paw Paw Bends of the Potomac. It was declared "A Wonder of the World," but it could only accommodate boats going in one direction in its 50-foot width. When two crafts met in the middle, arguments would ensue—for hours or even days on the few occasions when neither one would back out. Boats piled up for miles, bets were made, and the section superintendent might have to resort to starting a smoky fire at the end of the tunnel. With remarkable speed disputes were settled and the tunnel cleared.

The canal soon found itself competing with the new east–west route of the Baltimore & Ohio Railroad. The end came in 1924 when extensive flood damage and massive loss of business to the B&O forced the canal to close. The Chesapeake & Ohio Canal National Historic Park preserves the mostly dry canal and Potomac River bank as an unbroken historic shoestring park for hiking, biking, fishing, and sightseeing.

From the parking area it is a level walk of 0.6 mile along the remnants of the canal to the tunnel entrance. Hikers should carry a flashlight in the tunnel. It's not that the towpath isn't in perfect shape—it is—but there are things to see inside, such as rope burns on the railing, vertical shafts, "weep" holes dripping underground water, and a snow-like mineral deposit on the walls caused by evaporating groundwater. The air in the tunnel feels cool in warm weather and warm during the colder months. Singing in the tunnel is recommended; the acoustics improve most voices.

Ranger-guided tours of the tunnel are held occasionally on Saturday and Sunday during the warmer months. Check with the National Park Service (nps.gov/choh) for the schedule. In addition to picnic sites, this area features tent campsites, pit toilets, and Potomac River put-ins for canoes and boats.

7

Historic Eastern Panhandle

Harpers Ferry to Berkeley Springs

General description: From historic Harpers Ferry on the Potomac River, this 45-mile drive crosses the Shenandoah Valley to the mountain spa of Berkeley Springs.

Special attractions: Harpers Ferry National Historical Park, historical Shepherdstown, Martinsburg, Berkeley Springs State Park, the Shenandoah Valley, wooded mountain ridges.

Location: Easternmost West Virginia. Harpers Ferry is about 15 miles west of Frederick, Maryland, on US 340, and about an hour's drive from Washington, D.C.

Driving route numbers: US 340, 522; WV 9, 45, 230.

Travel season: All year.

Camping: Primitive state campground in Sleepy Creek Wildlife Management Area west of Hedgesville. Private campgrounds near Harpers Ferry and 10 miles north of Martinsburg in Falling Waters.

Services: Gasoline, restaurants, and lodging are readily available in most towns.

Nearby attractions: Harpers Ferry Toy Train Museum, Charles Town race track, Antietam National Battlefield Park, Chesapeake & Ohio Canal National Historic Park, Leetown Science Center, Cacapon Resort State Park.

The Route

Jutting eastward from the body of the state, the cosmopolitan Eastern Panhandle lies closer to the nation's capital and the Virginia and Maryland suburbs than it does to most of West Virginia. It looks more like a battered teapot spout than a "panhandle," but that is the term used for this peculiarly shaped region, cradled between Virginia and Maryland and bordered by the winding Potomac River along its northern and western edge.

Harpers Ferry, the starting point for this 45-mile drive, is the easternmost point in West Virginia. From here, the drive heads west through the Eastern Panhandle, crossing the West Virginia portion of the Shenandoah Valley farmlands, through the historic towns of Shepherdstown and Martinsburg. The drive then enters the Valley and Ridge province, climbing and descending several small ridges to end at the spas of Berkeley Springs.

The drive can easily be made in a few hours, but the many points of historic and scenic interest may entice you to linger along the way. Scenic Route 6, from Berkeley Springs to Paw Paw can be combined with this drive for a one-day trip.

The Eastern Panhandle was the first part of West Virginia to be settled by Europeans. When most of the state was still an unknown mountain wilderness, the towns of Harpers Ferry, Shepherdstown, Martinsburg, and Charles Town had

Historic Eastern Panhandle

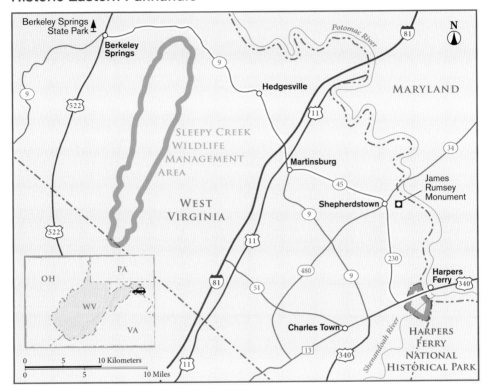

booming economies. This section's proximity to the nation's capital makes it the fastest growing area of the state today.

History lies around virtually every bend. George Washington relaxed from his surveying duties in the soothing natural spas of Berkeley Springs. The steamboat was invented in Shepherdstown in 1787, some 20 years before Robert Fulton steamed up the Hudson River. The Civil War was born at Harpers Ferry after John Brown's failed raid to free the slaves focused the nation's attention on the moral issue of slavery. Three states—Virginia, West Virginia, and Maryland—and two rivers—the Potomac and the Shenandoah—come together at Harpers Ferry. Both rivers have cut yawning gaps through the Blue Ridge Mountains, passes that have provided level travel routes east and west for more than 200 years. In fact, trains still stop here: A growing commuter community makes the daily hour-long commute to and from Washington, D.C.

The Blue Ridge range continues south into Virginia, culminating in the much higher peaks along Skyline Drive in Shenandoah National Park and the Blue

Ridge Parkway. These drives, plus some 20 others in the Old Dominion state, are described in the FalconGuide *Scenic Routes & Byways Virginia,* also published by Globe Pequot Press.

The most picturesque approach to Harpers Ferry is from Frederick, Maryland via US 340. This route descends into the Potomac River valley, crosses the river into Virginia, and a mile later crosses the Shenandoah River at its confluence with the Potomac to enter West Virginia. Both bridge crossings provide sweeping panoramas of the wide waterways and the steep, rocky slopes on either side; the Virginia portion has views across the Potomac to the town of Harpers Ferry, where buildings hug the flat ground along the river and climb steplike up the hillsides.

Because parking is limited in Harpers Ferry, most motorists park at the visitor center on US 340 about a mile west of the historic area and take a National Park Service bus into the historic area. There is a small entrance fee.

Harpers Ferry National Historical Park

Harpers Ferry (historicharpersferry.com) is named for John Harper, who operated a ferry service across both rivers in the mid-1700s. Today the town is part of **Harpers Ferry National Historical Park** (nps.gov/hafe) and has been restored to look much as it did in 1860 at the brink of the Civil War. Then it was a thriving rail and trade center with 3,000 residents, including an active community of 150 free blacks, many of whom were skilled and prosperous craftsmen such as masons and blacksmiths.

Many restored buildings now serve as small museums and exhibit areas; others are privately owned shops and restaurants. It is the largest single tourist draw in West Virginia. A good place to begin touring the town is at the National Park Service's information center on Shenandoah Street, where rangers answer questions and distribute maps that lead to such sites as the armory house that served as John Brown's fort during the abolitionist's raid. Across the street, the John Brown Museum chronicles the raid, capture, and hanging. Other programs depict the achievements of the African-American community, the birth of the National Association for the Advancement of Colored People (NAACP), and the town's role as an early US manufacturing center.

Several short hikes in this hilly town give you rewarding views for a certain amount of effort. Harpers Ferry is only 280 feet above sea level and the lowest point in West Virginia. A 5-minute stroll up the stone steps from High Street brings you to Jefferson Rock for a view that Thomas Jefferson declared was "worth a voyage across the Atlantic." For even more of a cardio workout, climb the Maryland Heights Trail, which gives you an outstanding view of the town and both rivers from the Maryland side of the Potomac.

Harpers Ferry sits at the confluence of the Shenandoah and Potomac Rivers.
West Virginia Department of Commerce, Stephen Shaluta

The town is also headquarters for the **Appalachian Trail Conservancy** (appalachiantrail.org); the **Appalachian Trail,** the world's best-known hiking path, runs through the center of town. The trail was born in regional planner Benton MacKaye's grief. When his wife died in 1921, he distracted himself by planning the Appalachian Trail (AT). He envisioned a 2,000-mile wilderness trail connecting forest camps, a "wilderness way through civilization . . . not a civilized way through the wilderness." Although much of the trail existed in rough footpaths, its full path between Georgia and Maine was not completed until 1937. Today the Appalachian Trail Conservancy (ATC) estimates that two million to three million people a year visit some portion of the AT, which—for northbound hikers— begins at Georgia's Springer Mountain and winds through 14 states to Maine's Mount Katahdin. The ATC helps coordinate the many volunteer and governmental agencies that maintain the trail.

Harpers Ferry is about the midpoint of the trailway, and thru-hikers consider it an important milestone. Most stop by ATC headquarters, the unofficial capital of the trail, to pay homage to the organization responsible for the trail's existence.

The trail passes through the Mountain State for only 4 miles, so in less than 2 hours you could have the right to brag that you hiked the Appalachian Trail all through West Virginia. South of Harpers Ferry, the trail climbs past Jefferson Rock to the ridgeline border between Virginia and West Virginia. Northbound hikers follow the AT across the Potomac into Maryland and along the Chesapeake & Ohio Canal for a few miles, where the trail turns north along low ridges into Pennsylvania.

Whitewater enthusiasts may enjoy a float or canoe trip down the Shenandoah Staircase, a 6-mile stretch with several class I to III rapids (mild to medium waves). These waters are tame compared with the world-class whitewater of West Virginia's New and Gauley Rivers, and they are very well suited for family groups. Fishing, tubing, rafting, canoeing, and kayaking are popular on both rivers. Trips can be arranged through **River Riders** (riverriders.com), located a few miles south of Harpers Ferry on Alstadts Hill Road; call (800) 326-7238 for information and reservations.

When you're ready to leave Harpers Ferry, go north on US 340. About 1 mile past the visitor center, turn right on WV 230. (A few miles straight ahead on US 340 is Charles Town, surveyed by George Washington in 1747 and named for his younger brother. The town, often confused with the state capital, Charleston, has several restored colonial buildings and is known for its racetrack, the Charles Town Race Track for thoroughbreds.)

WV 230 is a two-lane, winding road that passes through the rolling farmland of the Shenandoah Valley. The rich limestone soil and gentle slopes help make this some of the most fertile land in the state for pastures, vegetable farms, and fruit orchards.

As you cruise along you may want to start harmonizing to the late John Denver's chart-breaking hit "Country Roads." Denver teamed with songwriter Bill Danoff to write the song after a visit to the Eastern Panhandle. The first line, "Almost heaven, West Virginia," is instantly recognized and linked to the Mountain State worldwide.

After 9 miles you reach **Shepherdstown** on the banks of the Potomac River. Established in 1734 by Thomas Shepherd, the town was incorporated in 1762 and calls itself the oldest town in West Virginia. Many of the beautifully restored colonial homes and shops have helped place the town on the National Register of Historic Places. Most notable is the Entler Hotel, built in stages from 1786 to 1815, and now home to the Historic Shepherdstown Museum.

In the 1780s George Washington commissioned Shepherdstown resident James Rumsey to help develop and manage navigation on the Potomac River. But engineer Rumsey was more interested in building and inventing than he was in administration. In December 1787, his small steam-powered piston engine propelled a boat upstream in the turgid Potomac at the astounding speed of 3 knots, about 3.5 miles per hour.

Shepherdstown's Opera House Theatre on German Street screens foreign films.

The First Steamboat

Rumsey planned a larger, commercial version of his steamboat, but he died before this project was fully materialized. Some 20 years later Robert Fulton, building on Rumsey's design, cruised his *Clermont* up the Hudson River in the first successful and commercially viable steamboat.

A replica of Rumsey's steamboat and other memorabilia of his life and work are on exhibit at the **Rumsey Steamboat Museum** behind the Entler Hotel. Several times each summer volunteers from the Rumseian Society fill the boilers, light the fire, and chug up and down the Potomac under a full head of steam.

The inventor is also memorialized at the **James Rumsey Monument** at the end of N. Mill Street. This small park overlooks the Potomac from a 100-foot bluff. The monument itself, a tall column topped with a globe of the earth, symbolizes the international importance of Rumsey's work.

Jay Hurley, who built the half-size, fully functional replica of Rumsey's steamboat, says the engine is identical to that of Rumsey's full-size boat. Hurley is proprietor of **O'Hurley's General Store** (ohurley.com), restored to look as it did in the early 1900s. Hurley's love of music has led to regular Thursday night jam sessions at O'Hurley's that attract as many as 50 musicians accompanying Hurley on his hammer dulcimer.

The post-and-beam chalets beside the Potomac River are travelers' first indication they've found a little Bavaria. Inside the central stone manor, they're enveloped by the warm, winey scent of German food. The **Bavarian Inn** has been a mainstay here since 1977.

At the north end of town is the attractive campus of Shepherd University, a state-funded university founded in 1872 and a center for the arts. Each July the college hosts the **Contemporary American Theater Festival** (catf.org), during which presentations of new American plays are staged.

The town's laid-back atmosphere today belies its strife-riven history. During the Revolutionary War, Shepherdstown supplied more troops to the patriotic cause than any other town of its size. During the Civil War, shallows in the Potomac made Shepherdstown a strategic river crossing. The town served as a massive hospital following the **Battle of Antietam** (known in the Confederacy as the Battle of Sharpstown), on September 17, 1862, in Sharpstown, Maryland, 5 miles north of Shepherdstown.

The Rumsey Monument in Shepherdstown honors the inventor of the steamboat.
West Virginia Department of Commerce, Stephen Shaluta

JAMES RUMSEY'S
BOAT

The Battle of Antietam

During this bloody one-day battle, Union General George McClellan's troops clashed with Confederate General Robert E. Lee's soldiers, resulting in more than 22,700 men killed, wounded, or missing in action. After the conflict, Shepherdstown was filled with dead, dying, and injured men. Perhaps because of the unselfish care and attention the area's residents gave to soldiers of both sides, it was spared the burning and destruction that devastated so many other towns during the Civil War.

Although neither side claimed a victory in this battle, it dissuaded General Lee from moving farther north into federal territory; he withdrew to the south in what was considered a strategic victory for the federal forces.

WV 230 ends in Shepherdstown and becomes WV 45, which twists and winds about 7 miles to Martinsburg. In the center of the West Virginia section of the Shenandoah Valley, **Martinsburg** has been an historic transportation, agricultural, and business center since colonial days.

Like Shepherdstown, the Martinsburg area was settled in the early 1700s. It soon became a hub for southern and western travelers who traversed the Valley Pike between Pennsylvania and Virginia. When the Baltimore & Ohio Railroad was built in the 1840s, the town continued to prosper. The wagon trails were succeeded by US 11 and I-81; the railroad remains, mostly as a freight line, but it maintains daily Amtrak and commuter service to Washington, D.C.

The Civil War decimated Martinsburg, mainly because of its railroad yards. Martinsburg changed sides at least 50 times, experiencing widespread destruction throughout town. Despite the extensive damage, many beautiful 18th- and 19th-century buildings have been preserved or restored.

The town today has 7 historic districts and numerous buildings on the National Historic Register. You can obtain detailed information and maps for walking and driving tours at the Martinsburg/Berkeley County Convention & Visitors Bureau at 115 N. Queen St. (see appendix).

Historic buildings of particular interest include the museum at the **Belle Boyd House,** the childhood home of the famous female Civil War spy, and the **B&O Roundhouse,** originally built in 1842 and destroyed several times by Confederate troops during the Civil War; Union troops had to repair the tracks themselves nine times after Confederates destroyed them. The present roundhouse dates from 1868; a portion of it still functions as the Amtrak depot.

The George Washington Heritage Trail

To continue the drive turn west (right) on WV 9 at the T intersection of WV 45 and WV 9 in Martinsburg. Follow WV 9 west through Martinsburg, crossing US 11 and I-81. In a few minutes you're out in the fields and sprawling farmsteads of the Shenandoah Valley. This 26-mile stretch from Martinsburg to Berkeley Springs is known as the **George Washington Heritage Trail** (washingtonheritage. trail.org); it follows the historic turnpike first used by Native Americans and then by early settlers.

As you approach the small town of Hedgesville, about 6 miles from Martinsburg, you climb a small hill and the road begins to gently curve. The hill, small by West Virginia standards, marks the boundary between the near-level Shenandoah Valley province and the more dramatic relief of the Ridge and Valley province.

Hilly terrain continues past Hedgesville. As you cross Apple Pie Ridge (next to Potato Hill), look for Ridge Road—it's across from Hedgesville's high school. Lifelong farmer L. Norman Dillon left Berkeley County the funds to start a farm museum to memorialize a disappearing way of life in this fast-growing county. The **Dillon Farm Museum** preserves some of the tools of the trade, including apple graders, milking machines, and hand plows. A quick look around the farm reveals sawmills, tractors, and harrows. This gear is put into action during the museum's fall and spring shows, which also feature old-fashioned food like homemade ice cream and apple butter.

After a few miles you pass the entrance to The Woods, known for its golfing and retirement community. For those who want a more rustic setting, nearby is the state-run Sleepy Creek Wildlife Management Area, where a primitive campground surrounds a 205-acre lake.

Make a few more tight curves past the nose of Sleepy Creek Mountain, wending your way west. The landscape takes a definite turn for the vertical as you head into the resort town of **Berkeley Springs.** Berkeley Springs State Park, really a square in the center of town, is located at the intersection with US 522. The area has been known for its spas and mineral baths since the first Native Americans sought relaxation here more than 300 years ago. George Washington surveyed the town as a young man. He so much enjoyed soaking in the warm waters that he bought property in town, and for more than 40 years—even while president—he returned here for relaxation. He also named the town Bath after the English spa, and that is still the legal name of the town today.

Bathing in the springs is still a prime attraction here, but shopping and sightseeing are also popular. The town is the beginning of Scenic Route 6, Berkeley Springs to Paw Paw; that drive describes the town and area. To learn more about Berkeley Springs, turn to that chapter.

8

Center State Ramble

A Covered Bridge, the Wildlife Center & Historic Helvetia

General description: A 71-mile drive on paved roads through the knobby hills of central West Virginia. It features small college towns, the West Virginia State Wildlife Center, a miner memorial, and the historic town of Helvetia.

Special attractions: The Philippi covered bridge and mummies, glass studios around Buckhannon, Sago Miners Memorial, the West Virginia State Wildlife Center, and the Swiss town of Helvetia.

Location: Central West Virginia, almost in the middle of the state, beginning at Philippi.

Driving route numbers: US 119; WV 20; CR 11, 46.

Travel season: All year, but some attractions may be closed or have reduced hours in winter. Heavy winter snow may close roads temporarily.

Camping: No camping along the drive itself, but full-service camping facilities at nearby state parks, including Holly River, Audra, Stonewall Jackson Lake, and Tygart Lake state parks and Kumbrabow State Forest for a total of more than 200 campsites. Buckhannon has several private campgrounds.

Services: All services are available in Philippi and Buckhannon. Gas is not available past Buckhannon, and lodging and restaurants are limited.

Nearby attractions: Most of the state parks mentioned above have swimming and fishing facilities and hiking trails. Grafton, north of Philippi, has a shrine to Anna Jarvis, the mother of Mother's Day, and her birthplace is a few miles south of Grafton toward Philippi.

The Route

The small towns of central West Virginia have a charm that reflects their pastoral location, friendly residents, and easy living. This 71-mile drive starts near the covered bridge and mummies of Philippi. You then head south to Buckhannon, home of West Virginia Wesleyan College, and continue to French Creek to view the bison, elk, river otters, and other animals of the West Virginia State Wildlife Center. From there you head through a corduroy of wooded hills and occasional coal mines to Helvetia, restored to look as it did when settled by Swiss immigrants in 1869. The drive gets more rugged beyond Helvetia, but with views to match the hills and curves. It ends at Mill Creek, on the same Tygart Valley River that flows under the **Philippi covered bridge** (philippi.org). All roads are paved two-lane.

This is a long drive with lots of side-trip possibilities. You can easily spend several hours at the Wildlife Center, at glass studios around Buckhannon, and in Helvetia. You may want to visit Philippi and Buckhannon and stay overnight in Buckhannon, the only place on the drive where motels are plentiful.

Center State Ramble

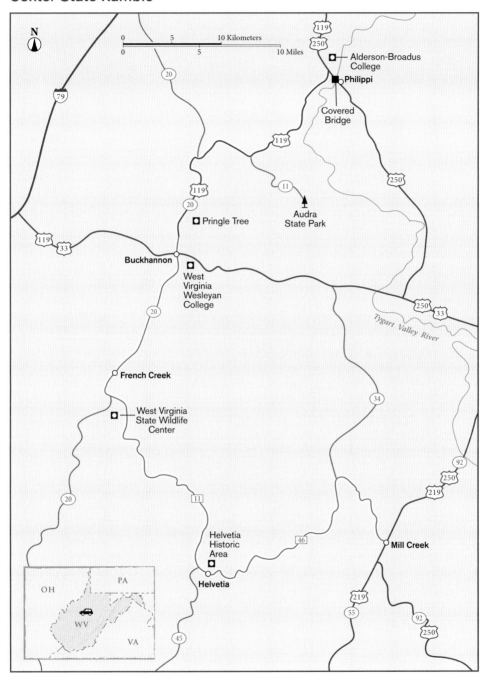

Philippi's arched covered bridge still serves traffic on a national highway.

Philippi is perhaps best known for its covered bridge, the longest, oldest, and arguably the prettiest in the state. Built in 1852, this handsome, 285-foot structure is still in use today; in fact it has the distinction of being the only two-lane covered bridge serving a US highway (US 250). The bridge was designed by Lemuel Chenoweth, whose improved Burr arch truss model was widely admired and frequently copied by other bridge builders. The bridge, at the edge of downtown Philippi, spans the Tygart Valley River.

The Battle of Philippi should stand out in the mind of every Civil War buff as the answer to the Civil War trivia question, "Where was the first land battle of the war?" The relatively bloodless battle, irreverently referred to as "the Philippi Races," resulted in a Union rout of Confederate forces threatening the Baltimore & Ohio Railroad.

On June 3, 1861, some 3,000 federal troops under the general command of Major General George McClellan and the immediate command of Colonel Benjamin Kelley and Colonel Ebenezar Dumont drove Colonel George Porterfield's 800 Confederates from the town. The only warning of the predawn surprise attack on camping Confederates came when a local housewife fired a few pistol shots at the Yankees. After getting out a few of their own shots at the advancing Union troops, the Southerners broke lines and ran frantically to the south, some still in their nightclothes. The Union victory propelled McClellan into the spotlight, and he was soon given command of all Union armies.

The first land battle featured several other firsts as well. This battle—or skirmish—lacked fatalities, but it was not without blood. A cannon ball slammed into the leg of a young Confederate soldier named James Hanger, an 18-year-old engineering student from Washington College. He became the first amputee of the Civil War when a Union surgeon performed surgery. Hanger returned to Virginia and whittled himself an artificial leg from barrel staves, putting a hinge at the knee. The design worked so well that Confederate brass commissioned him to manufacture the "Hanger limb" for other wounded Civil War veterans. He patented the prosthesis in 1871 and founded a company that is still a market leader in artificial limbs.

Chenoweth's bridge survived the battle plus several floods and fires over the years, but a fire in 1989 almost destroyed it. Using Chenoweth's original plans, craftsmen and engineers carefully restored the bridge. Today it maintains its original appearance, including the yellow poplar exterior, and is still structurally sound for modern usage.

The Mummies of Philippi

You can learn more about the bridge and the Civil War battle in the **Barbour County Historical Society Museum** (philippi.org), in a restored 1911 railroad depot beside the bridge. But many visitors to the museum are more interested in an exhibit in the tiled back room, **the Philippi mummies.** The mummies are two unidentified women who spent much of their short lives hidden away in the West Virginia Lunatic Asylum in nearby Weston. After their deaths in 1888, their bodies were obtained by Graham Hamrick, a local resident and part-time undertaker. Hamrick had invented a mummification process that he had already applied successfully to squirrels and vegetables.

The two corpses gave Hamrick the opportunity to apply his preservative methods to humans. He was so pleased with the results that he applied for and was granted a patent for his mummification process. For their part, the ladies went on a worldwide tour as the Hamrick Mummies with P. T. Barnum in 1891. Old records suggest that Hamrick also preserved a baby's body, but that disintegrated when the Tygart flooded in 1985. The mummified women were also damaged, and some say they were laid out on the post office lawn to dry. Although some object to the women being on display, the museum curator prefers to think of their exhibition as "a very long wake."

On the bluff to the north of town is the campus of Alderson-Broadus College, a leading school for the training of physicians' assistants and other medical personnel. Smaller than many high schools, with an enrollment of about 800, A-B, as it is called on campus, was moved from Winchester, Virginia, to Clarksburg, West Virginia, before settling down in Philippi in 1901. Downtown Philippi contains several historical buildings, most notably the imposing Barbour County Courthouse.

From Philippi drive south on US 119 through gently rolling farmland and woods. Relief here is low, with no major grades or curves. Nearby is **Audra State Park** (audrastatepark.com), a favorite place for kayaking, picnicking, hiking, and swimming in the Middle Fork River.

At Home in the Pringle Tree

US 119 is joined by WV 20 about 9 miles south of Philippi. Continue south (left) on US 119/WV 20. About 18 miles from Philippi look for small county signs to the **Pringle Tree.** A few hilly miles off the highway to the left, the current tree is the third-generation descendant of a huge, hollow sycamore that served as home and refuge for two deserters from the French and Indian War. Brothers John and Samuel Pringle deserted the British army at Fort Pitt (Pittsburgh) in 1761, set off through the wilderness, and then began winter housekeeping in the hollow tree, living on game and forage beside the Buckhannon River. Their room in the hollow trunk was reputed to be more than 11 feet wide.

Several years later, when they learned the war was over, they returned to civilization. Their enthusiasm for the area helped attract permanent settlers to this remote western region. The spreading sycamore at the site today is a smaller reminder of the giant sycamores that once were found across the state.

The town of **Buckhannon** (buckhannonwv.org) is about 1 mile past the Pringle Tree turnoff. To continue on the drive, cross under US 33 and continue south on WV 20. (US 119 turns west on US 33.) The history of this area has long been linked with the manufacture of fine glassware. Although most of the factories have closed in this age of plastics, a Buckhannon artisan is following his heart to continue the craft. You can watch glassblower **Ron Hinkle** (ronhinkle.com) at work in his studio, where he interacts with visitors as he handcrafts each piece. Learn about the ancient process of glassmaking and gain a special appreciation for the "magic of glass." You can also browse Ron's artistic creations in his gallery. The studio and gallery are located south of Buckhannon. Drive south on WV 20 to Sago Road, then follow the Hinkle Glass signs. Call (304) 472-7963 for information and hours.

You may want to take a few moments in Buckhannon to visit the tree-shaded, Georgian-style campus of **West Virginian Wesleyan College** (wvwc.edu), founded in 1890. At the campus center is the Wesley Chapel, easily spotted by its imposing steeple. With 1,600 seats, the chapel is the largest in the state; its huge, 1,500-pipe organ is easily heard from all seats. Also on campus is the Sleeth Art Gallery.

Buckhannon itself is undergoing a bit of a renaissance as a younger generation of entrepreneurs builds parks and takes over historic late 19th-century

The Buckhannon River runs past the Sago Mine.

buildings, making attractive restaurants, galleries, and shops. Architect Bryson Von Nostrand has created a small restaurant, intimate music venue, and the Lascaux Micro-Theatre, named for a French cave, underneath his offices. This 40-seat underground theater screens foreign and independent films every Friday night; patrons can, and often do, bring wine to share.

In May, to top off the local harvest, Buckhannon celebrates the week-long **Strawberry Festival**. The town comes out for the eats—strawberries, strawberries with cream, strawberry cobbler, strawberry pie, and more strawberries—and to watch as the Strawberry Queen leads a parade down Strawberry Lane. The festival is usually held the third weekend in May, but check their website (visit buckhannon.org) for specifics.

As you leave town on WV 20, you pass numerous well-maintained Victorian style homes interspersed with moderate suburban sprawl. Ron Hinkle's studio is located about 4 miles south of town off Sago Road, or CR 22—on the left, look for the signs. He's appropriately located on Glassblower Road off Sago Road. You may remember Sago—yes, this is the same road that leads to the nearby Sago Mine, where 12 good miners died on January 2, 2006. The road has been renamed Coal Miners' Memorial Roadway as it follows the winding Buckhannon River to the now-closed mine and Sago Baptist Church. Beside the Sago church a small park commemorates the miners. A 6-foot memorial is etched with the photograph of each man who died and bears a quote from the note miner Martin Toler Jr. left for his family: "We'll see you on the other side." A bench in front of the statue is dedicated to the sole survivor of the Sago Mine disaster, Randal McCloy.

The State Wildlife Center

At French Creek, about 12 miles from Buckhannon, turn left on CR 11 at the well-marked entrance to the **West Virginia State Wildlife Center** (wvdnr.gov/wildlife). The facility, operated by the West Virginia Division of Natural Resources, displays native wildlife of the state in 300 acres of woods and meadows. Mountain lions, gray wolves, black bear, fishers, bald eagles, deer, and other animals may be viewed in natural habitats. A special river otter exhibit lets you see swimming animals from both above and below the water level. Animals no longer found in West Virginia, such as bison and elk, graze in open fields. A 1.25-mile loop walking trail passes along the wooded exhibit area.

The center was originally opened as a game farm in 1923. As conservationist thinking changed, the idea of a game farm went out of favor, and the current wildlife center was established as more of a zoo in 1986. You can visit any time, but an admission fee is charged from April 1 to October 31 when the visitor center is open.

When you leave the center parking lot, turn right (east) on CR 11. The 20 miles to Helvetia are sparsely populated and more hilly than the first part of the drive. You'll also pass the pipes and well heads of several gas wells. As you cross from Upshur County to Randolph County, the route number changes to CR 46.

Switzerland in West Virginia

Helvetia (helvetiawv.com) is a little bit of Switzerland preserved and hidden in the hills of West Virginia. The town was settled in 1869 by Swiss and German immigrants, whose descendants can still be overheard speaking high German. As the farm community grew to 1,000 strong, they chose the name Helvetia, the Latin term for Switzerland.

Today there are only about 60 year-round residents, but the Swiss pride and heritage live on. Through their efforts, at least 10 historic buildings have been preserved, and the entire village has been placed on the National Register of Historic Places. The buildings include the original one-room schoolhouse, a settler's cabin, a small inn, a church, a dance hall, and a library. The general store and post office, Kultur Haus, includes a museum of masks created for Helvetia's rowdy

Helvetia's Honey Haus is part of the restored Swiss village in the heart of West Virginia woodland.

pre-Lenten ball, Fasnacht. The building also includes 5 simple rooms for overnight lodging. The buildings, clustered together with a restaurant, cheese store, and honey house on the banks of a gurgling stream, can be visited with a minimum of walking. Entrance to all buildings is free.

The townspeople honor their heritage with song, dance, and frivolity. There are square dances during the warmer months. The Helvetia Fair, held during the second weekend in September, celebrates the harvest with a cheese festival and animal parade; Fasnacht, the Saturday before Ash Wednesday, memorializes the end of winter with a costume ball and the burning of Old Man Winter in effigy.

If you're feeling hungry, the **Hütte Restaurant**, serves local food prepared in genuine Swiss style. If you're lucky enough to be there for Sunday brunch or lunch, be sure to order the Bernerplatte, a bountiful buffet of Swiss culinary masterpieces. Dishes, all homemade, include stout soup, homemade Helvetia sausage, sauerkraut, sauerbraten, Helvetian Swiss cheese, and a tasty variety of breads and desserts. But be forewarned: This is the only restaurant for at least 25 miles, and it is popular.

The Hütte is an authentically Swiss restaurant in Helvetia.

When you leave town, continue east on WV 46. This section of the drive is the most rugged, with higher hills, steeper grades, and more curves. The hills soon turn into distinct ridges, with distant views from the high points. At the bottom of one valley is a coal mine and loading station on a railroad spur.

The drive concludes about 21 miles from Helvetia with a steep descent to the junction with US 219/250 in the town of Mill Creek.

9

Canaan Valley Loop

Through the East's Highest Valley

General description: A 45-mile loop drive in the Monongahela National Forest through the mountains and wetlands of Canaan Valley, the highest valley of its size east of the Rockies.

Special attractions: Canaan Valley Resort State Park, Canaan Valley National Wildlife Refuge, and Blackwater Falls State Park.

Location: Eastern-central West Virginia, south of Morgantown.

Driving route numbers: US 219; WV 32, 72.

Travel season: All year. Snows are heavy in winter; WV 72 may close temporarily. Many attractions are seasonal.

Camping: Canaan Valley Resort State Park is open all year and has 34 tent or trailer sites with all facilities. Blackwater Falls State Park's campgrounds are open May through Nov and have 65 tent or trailer sites, about half with all facilities.

Services: Food and fuel are available year-round in Davis and along WV 32 and US 219. Motels, ski resort, condominiums, and lodges in the state parks provide numerous overnight accommodations year-round. Reservations are recommended, particularly during ski season and when fall foliage is at its peak. There are no services along WV 72.

Nearby attractions: Fairfax Stone and Dolly Sods.

The Route

Canaan (pronounced Keh NANE) Valley is the highest major valley east of the Rockies and the largest wetland complex in West Virginia. Surrounded by mountains, its diverse habitats include dense deciduous and conifer forests, swiftly flowing streams, fragile bogs, and wetlands.

Canaan Valley is a place of quiet beauty where deer are tame enough to eat out of your hand—but don't do it; feeding them is illegal, and unhealthy for the deer. The bold deer are among the 290 animal species that live here; a biodiverse community of almost 600 species of plants thrive in this high, cool paradise as well. Rimmed by mountains, the bowl-like valley receives 150 to 200 inches of snow each year, and with an average elevation of 3,200 feet at the valley floor, its climate is more like that of New England than most of West Virginia.

With so much beauty and so much snow, it's not surprising that the valley is a four-season destination. Within its bounds, visitors can entertain themselves at 2 state parks, a national wildlife refuge, a downhill ski resort, and a cross-country ski facility. Popular activities include hiking, birding, golfing, mountain biking, skiing, and snowboarding, as well as plain old relaxing as the sunset fades slowly over the high bogs.

Canaan Valley Loop

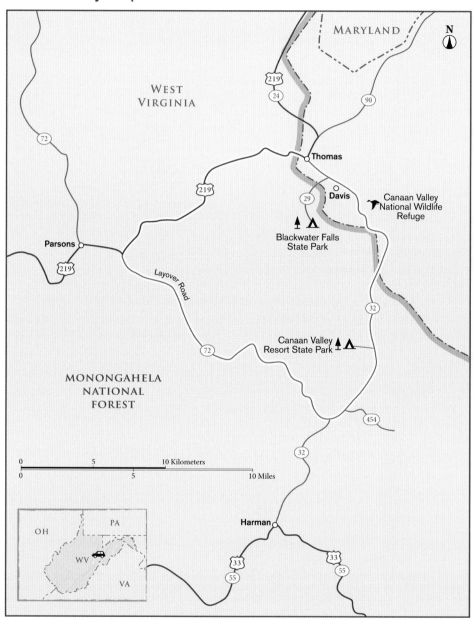

MARYLAND

N

WEST
VIRGINIA

219

24

90

72

Thomas

219

29   Davis

Canaan Valley
National Wildlife
Refuge

Parsons

Blackwater Falls
State Park

219

Layover Road

32

72

Canaan Valley
Resort State Park

MONONGAHELA
NATIONAL
FOREST

454

0   5   10 Kilometers
0   5   10 Miles

32

PA

OH

WV

Harman

VA

33

55

33

55

The valley was named "Canaan" by settlers in the 1700s who thought they had found a piece of the biblical promised land in the New World. It was little known until the 1850s, when the name and the valley were popularized by author and illustrator David Hunter Strother, better known by his pen name of Porte Crayon. His series of writings and drawings of the mountains of West Virginia in *Harper's New Monthly Magazine* made him the most celebrated travel writer of his time.

This loop drive can be started from several entry points. For our purposes, it will begin at the southern tip of the loop at the intersection of WV 32 and 72. The drive follows WV 32 north about 15 miles through the center of this pretty valley, an uncharacteristic West Virginia flat spot that seems perpetually bathed in a soft filtered light. There's just so much sky here. **Canaan Valley Resort State Park** (canaanresort.com) sprawls over the meadow on your left, its new sporting-clay shooting range hidden in the forest and its renovated lodge featuring rooms with panoramic views of this magical valley. At Davis, about 5 miles north, a short sidetrack to gorgeous Blackwater Falls State Park (blackwaterfalls.com) is in order. At the historic coal-mining town of Thomas, the drive turns west on US 219 for 12 miles, passing the turnoff to the famed **Fairfax boundary stone** (wvstateparks .com) at the source of the North Branch of the Potomac River. At WV 72, outside the town of Parsons, turn left (southeast) for an 18-mile drive south on a true "road less traveled" (although it is paved) through high country west of the valley to the starting point at WV 32. This totals about 45 miles, but you will probably add 8 to 10 miles for trips off the main drive. The entire route lies within sight of the Monongahela National Forest.

From the starting point, drive north on WV 32 through an open valley surrounded by mountains. Within 2.5 miles, you come to the entrance of Canaan Valley Resort State Park, a premier-resort state park that has just undergone extensive renovations. Open year-round, the park runs Canaan Valley Ski Resort, where skiers and snowboarders ride chairlifts to the mountaintop and schuss down groomed slopes. Cross-country skiers and snowshoers can glide through the quiet forests across miles of trails. Aprés-ski activities include soothing sore muscles in the hot tubs at the spa, swimming in the indoor pool, or just relaxing in the newly renovated lodge.

The Walk Between the Parks

When the snow melts and the wildflowers start to bloom, Canaan Valley's cross-country trails turn into hiking trails. The wheelchair-accessible Abe Run Boardwalk at Canaan Valley Resort State Park gives virtually all visitors a chance to see deer, beaver, swamp sparrows, cedar waxwings, and perhaps a muskrat or two in the evening. A popular day hike is the "Walk Between the Parks," an 8.5-mile, one-way hike between Canaan Valley Resort and Blackwater Falls State Park. Other hikes, including the 330-mile Allegheny Trail, connect to the trail system in the adjoining Monongahela National Forest.

The warmer months bring a variety of scheduled activities, from wildflower pilgrimages to bird watching to astronomy weekends. Stop at the nature center to find out what is currently offered. Golfers can indulge in scenic driving of another sort at the championship 18-hole course, followed by a dip in the outdoor Olympic-size swimming pool.

When you're ready to leave the state park, return to WV 32 and turn north (left). Roads to the right will lead to **White Grass Ski Touring Center** (whitegrass.com), as well as to private condominiums. Also off to the right are the high marshes, wetlands, and high country of the **Canaan Valley National Wildlife Refuge,** with flora and ecology almost like that of Canada.

Established in 1994 as the country's 500th national wildlife refuge, its 17,000 acres protect numerous plant communities thriving in these high elevation marshes since the end of the Pleistocene ice age. Each spring and fall these marshes—the second largest freshwater wetlands in the US—provide feeding grounds for enormous numbers of migrating wading birds, shorebirds, and waterfowl. It is also a major breeding area for the American woodcock.

Development of this wild area has been minimal, and most visitors hike over the few unmarked trails. You can plan your visit in advance by calling or contacting the refuge (see the appendix). One popular trail begins on Freeland Road near the White Grass Ski Touring Center; another starts from Old Timberline Road near Cortland. None of these roads is shown on the map in this book; ask locally for detailed directions.

Continue on WV 32 to the town of **Davis,** about 15 miles from the starting point. At an elevation of about 3,200 feet, Davis is the highest incorporated town east of the Mississippi; its wide streets and wooden, false storefronts give it a Western look. Natural air-conditioning made it popular as a summer resort more than 100 years ago. It's even more popular today with skiers, hikers, golfers, anglers, fall leaf peepers, and others who seek relaxation in the colorful cafes, restaurants, galleries, and craft shops.

Blackwater Falls & Gorge

One of the main reasons people come to Davis lies a mile west of town on the left: **Blackwater Falls State Park** (blackwaterfalls.com). The crown jewel of the park, 60-foot Blackwater Falls, cascades into the 8-mile-long gorge of the Blackwater River.

Canaan Valley receives at least 150 inches of snow each winter.

Blackwater Falls cascades more than 60 feet into Blackwater Canyon.

The world first learned about Blackwater Falls in the mid-1800s from the vivid descriptions and sketches of magazine writer and illustrator Porte Crayon. Reaching the falls in his day was an arduous trip by foot or horseback on rough trails over rugged hills and canyons.

Today the falls are accessible via a wooden boardwalk. As you descend the numerous steps, the roar of the water grows louder at every viewpoint, reaching a crescendo at the base of the falls. Watching the water pour over the rocks has a mesmerizing effect on some visitors, who may sit here and reflect for hours.

Below the falls, the Blackwater River roars through an 8-mile canyon. The river gets its name from its tea-colored hue, a result of the tannic acid leached from decaying vegetation, mostly hemlock leaves and red spruce needles.

Other hiking trails, including the "Walk Between the Parks," wind through the thick woods back to Canaan Valley State Park. Most popular and easiest is the paved, wheelchair-accessible Gentle Trail, which leads to an observation deck overlooking the falls. The undeveloped Blackwater Canyon Rail Trail that follows the gorge along an old narrow gauge logging railroad requires a higher fitness level. Winter brings a quiet solitude of green and white as heavy snows cover the trails, and the park becomes a ski-touring center. A well-equipped ski shop provides equipment and rentals.

Open all year, the lodge and restaurant offer diners and overnight guests scenic views into the canyon. A variety of year-round nature programs, guided hikes, and other events, such as the Septemberfest Senior Fling, may add interest to your visit. A campsite is open during the warmer months.

When you return to WV 32, continue north (left). In less than 2 miles, you will come to **Thomas,** a former coal town noted for its historic district and the **Purple Fiddle restaurant** (purplefiddle.com), which is really a restaurant, music venue, occasional soup kitchen, and community hub. At the intersection in Thomas, turn left (west) on US 219, a major two-lane highway. This section of US 219 follows part of the Seneca Trail or Warriors Path, a Native American footpath from upstate New York to the southern mountains. Efforts are being made to preserve parts of the path before it is swallowed up by development.

As you ascend Backbone Mountain, you will see 345-foot wind turbines sprouting out of the ridge. If you pull off on Sugarlands Road to the right, you'll be able to hear the soft paddling sound of a nearby turbine as it slices through the wind. There are some 166 turbines lining the top of this north–south ridge for miles.

A 4-mile downgrade to the Cheat River Valley begins about 8 miles past Thomas. If you need gasoline, food, or other services, stay on US 219 another mile to reach the town of Parsons, as you won't find much on WV 72. Otherwise, turn left (west) on WV 72 for a hilly, winding ride; note that it is not suited for large RVs.

A Layover Road

WV 72 borders a popular fishing creek for a few miles, passing through the hamlets of Elk and Hendricks. This part of the route gives you a classic West Virginia road-driving experience: the layover road. The road becomes so narrow that in places the paved portion is not wide enough for two vehicles to pass. This means that when you encounter an oncoming vehicle, both of you will pull over—layover—to the right as far as possible. The left wheels of both vehicles will be on the paved portion; the right wheels will be in the dirt. This is the layover position. It is considered good manners to wave to the other driver as you go by, but only your index finger is required.

After a few miles the road becomes very twisty and climbs a steep grade from the creek. The heavy woods give way to numerous open fields and grazing lands, too vertical for cultivation. After passing the small settlement of Red Creek, both WV 72 and the drive end at the starting point, the junction with WV 32.

10

Through Greenland Gap

Moorefield to Scherr

General description: A 22-mile drive along a wide river valley, over Patterson Creek Mountain, and through a narrow gap between the towering cliffs of Greenland Gap.

Special attractions: Greenland Gap's cliffs, birds, and other wildlife; the Moorefield historic district; and the wide valley of the South Branch of the Potomac River.

Location: East-central West Virginia.

Driving route numbers: US 220/WV 28; CR 1, 2, 3, 3-3, 5.

Travel season: All year. Migrating birds are best seen in Greenland Gap in early May and after cold fronts pass through in autumn. Rhododendrons reach their peak in July. Winter has a special charm in Greenland Gap, but travel may be restricted for a day or two after snowstorms.

Camping: Riverside Cabins & RV Park, Moorefield.

Services: All services are available in Moorefield.

Nearby attractions: Spruce Knob, Dolly Sods, Seneca Rocks, and the Potomac Eagle excursion train in Romney.

The Route

This short drive heads northeast from Moorefield along the valley of the South Branch of the Potomac River to cross the gentle slopes of Patterson Creek Mountain. From there, it passes through a Nature Conservancy preserve at Greenland Gap along the North Fork of Patterson Creek to end at the little town of Scherr.

Moorefield, like many towns in eastern West Virginia, changed hands numerous times during the Civil War. The historic district preserves several old buildings, including McCoy's Grand Theatre (mccoysgrand.com) and the Hardy County Courthouse. This is the heart of West Virginia's poultry country, and the scent of fried chicken hangs over town during the workday at the Pilgrim's Pride chicken processing plant. Long, low chicken houses dot the wide valley, and an annual West Virginia Poultry Festival has been held here in late July ever since 1943. The five-day event includes a parade, beauty contest, turkey trot, and, of course, lots of fried chicken.

From Moorefield, drive north on US 220/WV 28, a wide two-lane road. This takes you along the broad valley of the South Branch of the Potomac River past prosperous dairy farms. This pastoral scene is framed by low-lying mountain ridges on both sides—the South Branch Mountain on the east and Patterson Creek Mountain on the left.

To the north, you can see where the South Branch of the Potomac narrows as it flows through Falling Springs Gap. The other side of this gap marks the

Through Greenland Gap

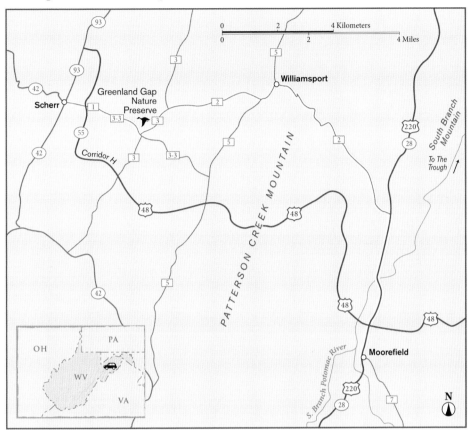

beginning of The Trough, a picturesque canyon known for its bald eagle nesting sites. You can tour the canyon from the popular Potomac Eagle Scenic Railroad, which departs from Romney in late April through November. Although it is not guaranteed, eagles are frequently seen in the canyon.

After crossing the South Branch of the Potomac, turn left (west) on Old Fields Road (CR 2) about 5 miles from Moorefield. This narrow, two-lane paved road rambles across the limestone plains through sheep and cattle pastures. After a few miles it climbs the gentle slopes of Patterson Creek Mountain.

A moderate descent down the other side ends at the stop sign in Williamsport at CR 5. Turn left (south). Go about 0.75 mile to Belle Babb Lane, a continuation of CR 2, and turn right (west). You will pass a 30-foot-high earthen embankment built for flood control along the North Fork of Patterson Creek.

At the stop sign at a fork in the road about 17.5 miles into your drive, bear left (south) on CR 3. In 0.5 mile, turn right on Greenland Gap Road (CR 3-3) into Greenland Gap Nature Preserve.

Into Greenland Gap

This short but spectacular 4-mile pass through Knobly Mountain is home to the **Greenland Gap Nature Preserve** (nature.org). The rocks here fold dramatically; the ridge itself is composed of whitish Tuscarora sandstone of the Silurian age. The entire gap is ringed by towering cliffs, which rise 800 feet above the cool, clear waters of the North Fork of Patterson Creek. The weather-resistant sandstone underlies most of the ridges and mountaintops throughout the Appalachian Mountains. This base nurtures the acid soil that produces lovely pink rhododendron blossoms in July.

As you enter the preserve, the open fields immediately give way to woods and dense thickets of rhododendron.

Less than 0.25 mile from the entrance, the road squeezes past rapids shooting through the mossy chasm. At Falls Gap, the clear waters tumble down a rock incline into the jade green pool below. Along the road are huge blocks of sandstone from the cliffs above.

A half mile ahead at the main parking area, 2 trails, one on each side of the road, lead hikers to the cliff tops for dramatic views. Warning: These trails are aerobically demanding, steep, and rocky.

To hike, park at the pull-off. The northside trail can be found by crossing the creek (stepping stones, no bridge) and walking down the old road until you see a 4-foot post on the left. The trail begins here. The southside trailhead is about 30 feet from the pull-off, on the same side of the gap as the main entrance sign. On warm summer and early autumn days, hundreds of turkey vultures and ravens can be spotted circling in the gap's warm updrafts; the rocky crags make an ideal place for these birds to lay their eggs earlier in the year.

Greenland Gap is one of more than a dozen nature preserves maintained by the West Virginia chapter of the Nature Conservancy. The cliff tops of this 255-acre preserve make superb viewing points to observe migrating neotropical birds flying north in early May or after a cold front passes through in early autumn. If you wander through the woods you may spot some white-tailed deer, wild turkeys, or even a black bear.

Besides being a West Virginia Natural Landmark, Greenland Gap is site of an April 1863 Civil War battle between about 1,500 Confederate soldiers and 87 Union soldiers, who had taken positions in a church and cabins at the west end of the gap. General William "Grumble" Jones and his cavalry were advancing through the gap when they encountered the Yankees. The Union men managed to hold off several assaults over four hours of fighting, but when the Confederates set the church on fire, they surrendered.

Moorefield changed hands many times in the Civil War and has a historic downtown.

Greenland Gap makes a beautiful cut through Knobly Mountain.

Greenland Gap Nature Preserve is open all year, but snow may temporarily close the road in winter.

When you leave the preserve, bear left on CR 1 in the hamlet of Greenland. You'll pass under West Virginia's new Corridor H expressway to the ski areas, known as WV 55 in this area. Several limestone quarries operated by the State Road Commission for road construction may make the road a bit dusty at this point. At the stop sign in Scherr (pronounced Shear), bear left and go 500 feet to WV 93 and the end of the drive. To return to Moorefield turn around and retrace your trip, or turn left on WV 93 to go to Petersburg and then Moorefield.

11

Lost River & Cacapon River

Clear Streams & Gentle Mountains

General description: A 55-mile drive that meanders along the headwaters of two crystal-clear streams through the broad mountains adjacent to the George Washington National Forest.

Special attractions: Lost River State Park, Capon Springs Resort, scenic river valleys, and rolling farmlands.

Location: Eastern West Virginia, about 20 miles west of Winchester and Front Royal, Virginia, and I-81.

Driving route numbers: CR 12, 14, 16; old WV 55, 259.

Travel season: All year.

Camping: The campground at Edward's Run Wildlife Management Area north of Capon Bridge has 6 year-round primitive sites. The George Washington National Forest seasonally maintains the Hawk Campground Area near Capon Springs and Trout Pond Campground near Lost River. A private campground, Big Ridge, adjoins Lost River State Park and is open seasonally.

Services: All services are available in most towns along the drive.

Nearby attractions: George Washington National Forest and Potomac Eagle Scenic Railroad.

The Route

Compared to the rugged ridges and crags of Seneca Rocks, Spruce Knob, and Dolly Sods, the northeastern section of the Potomac Highlands is a land of gentle mountains and placid streams. Old farms and villages, streams and forested hills create a varied patchwork along this beautiful stretch of the Cacapon and Lost Rivers.

This drive explores the headwaters of both rivers, passing a historic spa, traversing a narrow valley, and yielding frequent views of distant mountains. The drive ends at one of West Virginia's outstanding state parks. Only 2 hours from the Washington, D.C., metropolitan area, the drive can easily be made as part of a day trip.

The route begins at the bridge in the town of Capon Bridge, about halfway between Winchester, Virginia, and Romney, West Virginia. Go south on CR 14, Cacapon River Road, just west of the iron truss bridge across the river on US 50.

As you leave town, look left at the first farm along the river for grazing llamas, burros, and ostrich-like emus. This is private property, but the animals are a delightful addition to the viewshed.

The route follows the clear-flowing Cacapon River, popular with anglers for its largemouth and smallmouth bass and catfish. Numerous fishing camps dot both sides of the river. Where the valley is wider, cattle, sheep, and horses graze

Lost River & Cacapon River

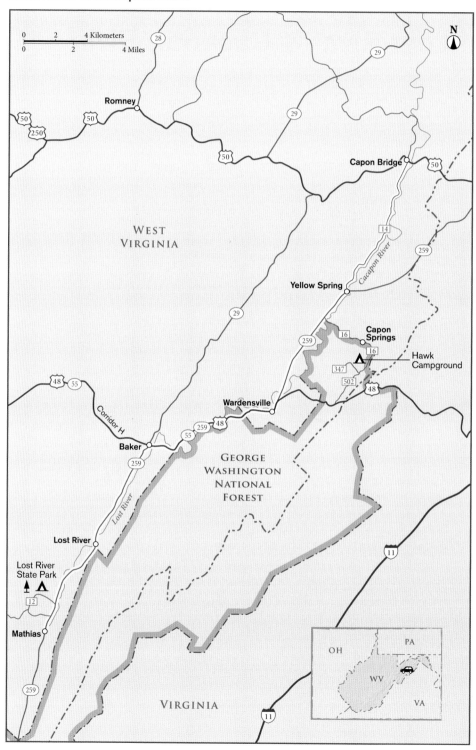

The Cacapon Valley has high limestone ledges and prosperous farms.

in front of prosperous-looking older farms. The steep ridge to the right with castle-like outcroppings of whitish rock is Cacapon Mountain. As the drive heads upstream to the headwaters of the Cacapon, the river gradually narrows.

At the intersection in Yellow Spring, about 10 miles from Capon Bridge, CR 14 ends. Bear right (south) on WV 259. Two miles south of this point, an old highway bridge is partially preserved as a fishing pier on the Cacapon. Just past the old bridge, turn left (east) on CR 16, Capon Springs Road. (The name "Capon" has nothing to do with altered chickens; it is a shortened version of "Cacapon," the American Indian name for the river.)

Capon Springs Resort

CR 16 leaves the Cacapon River and winds along a small creek through thick woods to the small settlement at **Capon Springs** (caponsprings.net). Continue straight at the intersection by the octagonal house to reach the historic springs and resort. (To the right is the Hawk Campground in the George Washington National Forest.)

The springs here were known to the American Indians and attracted European settlers in the late 1700s. In 1849, a 4-story hotel was built to cater to the well-to-do who came to enjoy the carbonated-lithium spring waters. The original hotel burned down in 1911, but the graceful Victorian-style buildings are authentic, built in the 1880s. Now a national registered historic district, these porched and pillared structures serve a family-oriented resort known for its mineral baths, fresh-from-the-garden meals, and casual atmosphere. The former Pavilion bathhouse has been converted to guest rooms, but the Hygeia Spa and Bath House remain.

When you leave Capon Springs, go back to WV 259, and turn south (left), leaving the Cacapon watershed. After a few miles the valley opens up, with distant views of Great North Mountain to the east. At the intersection with old WV 55, bear south and west (right) on old WV 55/259. The new WV 55, part of the Corridor G freeway to the ski resorts, is fast, but not nearly as interesting as it zooms far above the valley on pylons with nary a glimpse of a creek or an identifiable tree.

South of Wardensville, cross a small ridge that divides the watershed of the Cacapon River from that of Lost River. After a short drive downhill you enter the picturesque gorge of Lost River. The river becomes "lost" after it flows into an underground channel northeast of Baker at a rocky spot known as "the Sinks" and reappears near Wardensville as the Cacapon. As you emerge from the gorge, note the old quarry where you can see the near-vertical beds of sandstone and limestone that were intensely folded as the mountains rose 250 million years ago.

At Baker turn left (south) on WV 259 where WV 55 continues straight. The Lost River flows through a flat valley, bordered on the left by steep wooded hills that mark the approximate boundary of Virginia's George Washington National Forest.

As you progress downstream the valley widens. The "Lost" theme continues as you pass through the small communities of Lost River and Lost City. Look for the sign to Lost River State Park just before Mathias. At the turn to the park you'll see the restored John Mathias Homestead, a rough-hewn, 2-story log cabin. Built in 1797, the house is the oldest in the county.

On to Lost River State Park

Turn right on CR 12 for a 4-mile drive to the wooded and hilly park. Most of **Lost River State Park** (lostriversp.com) originally was the property of General Henry "Light Horse Harry" Lee, father of Confederate General Robert E. Lee. The elder Lee received the land as a grant for his military leadership during the Revolutionary War. He built a cabin as a summer retreat beside Howard's Lick, a sulphuric (supposedly healing) spring that is also known as Lee White Sulphur Spring. The original foundation has stone blocks so true they look as if they were cut by machine. Antique tools and furniture fill the rooms of the Lee House. Several horseback and hiking trails now lead to the spring and the white 2-story cabin, which is open summer weekends.

Other trails in the park lead to scenic overlooks, including 3,200-foot-high Cranny Crow Overlook, with its commanding views of surrounding ridges. The park, including 9 rental cottages, is open year-round. Seasonal activities include

Lost River State Park's main office and many cabins were constructed by the Civilian Conservation Corps in the 1930s.

naturalist programs, horseback riding, swimming, and shopping in the park gift shop. A private campground adjacent to the park is available during the warmer months.

The drive ends at the park. You can retrace your route, follow the signs to go to Moorefield, or return to Mathias and follow WV 259 south to New Market, Virginia, and I-81.

12

Dolly Sods Scenic Area

On Top of the Allegheny Front

General description: This 30-mile drive within Monongahela National Forest climbs 2,500 feet up the steep Allegheny Front on a dirt road to magnificent views at the Dolly Sods, a windswept high plain with a climate and flora similar to northern Canada.

Special attractions: The Allegheny Front, the highland plain, unusual plants, one-sided spruces, unsurpassed 50-mile scenic views, hikes, and migrating hawks and other birds.

Location: The Potomac Highlands of eastern West Virginia about 10 miles west of Petersburg.

Driving route numbers: CR 45-4; FS 19, 75.

Travel season: Spring through autumn, but watch the weather. Severe thunderstorms, gale-force winds, and thick fog can move in quickly. Snow can occur any time from early autumn to late spring, and the road is not plowed. Check with the Forest Service

if you have any doubts about conditions or the weather. Migrating songbirds and hawks are best viewed from mid-August through mid-October.

Camping: The Red Creek Campground has 12 primitive sites with pit toilets. Canaan Valley State Park (Scenic Route 9) near the northern end of this drive has about 35 fully equipped campsites. Seneca Shadows Campground, 1 mile south of Seneca Rocks, has about 80 campsites.

Services: None. Make sure you have enough gas. If you want, bring a lunch to eat at the Red Creek Campground picnic site.

Nearby attractions: The drive lies in the middle of some of the most superb scenic and recreational areas of Monongahela National Forest. Nearby are hiking, Seneca Rocks, Spruce Knob, cave tours, and Canaan Valley Resort State Park.

The Route

The Dolly Sods lie on the eastern edge of the Allegheny Plateau at an elevation of about 4,050 feet. The high windswept plains and one-sided spruces of the Dolly Sods are a unique piece of the boreal forest in West Virginia, with a climate and plant life similar to parts of northern Canada. The Dolly Sods also provide some of the best views in the state, overlooking ridge after ridge to the east.

East of the Dolly Sods and some 2,500 feet lower lies the western boundary of the Valley and Ridge province. Connecting the Allegheny Plateau and the Valley and Ridge is a prominent escarpment, the Allegheny Front, which runs northeast–southwest through much of West Virginia.

From the starting point of the drive, at the intersection of WV 28 and FS 19, you traverse about 7 miles of gravel road to climb more than 2,500 feet up the Allegheny Front. From there it is another 7 miles on level gravel roads to Bear Rocks, the most scenic part of the Dolly Sods. From Bear Rocks, you can continue the drive to Canaan Valley near Canaan Valley State Park for a total distance of

Dolly Sods Scenic Area

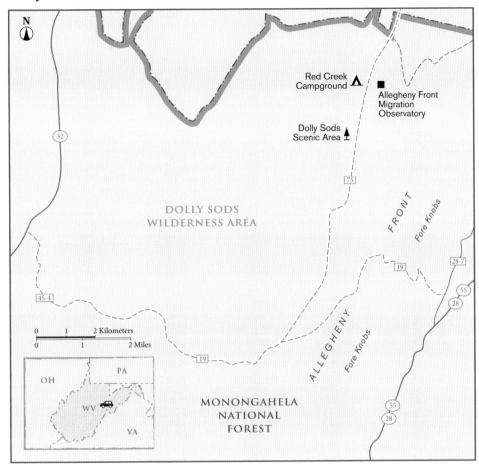

about 30 miles. Or you can take an optional shorter loop that returns to the start of the drive for a total drive of about 25 miles. Whatever way you go from Bear Rocks, it will mostly be on dirt and gravel roads with plenty of downhill stretches. The entire route lies almost entirely within the Monongahela National Forest.

You can make the drive in any vehicle, but make sure the brakes and the cooling system are in good condition. Do not attempt the drive in winter or in stormy weather in any season. Conditions can deteriorate quickly at high elevations. Check with the US Forest Service about the road and weather conditions. The grades are steep in places, but there are few curves, and the gravel road is wide, with plenty of places to pull over, but not everyone is comfortable driving mountainous gravel roads. If you are confident of your abilities and your vehicle, the drive is well worth your time; the Dolly Sods is a unique, high-altitude ecosystem seen no place else in the continental US.

The intersection of WV 28 and the beginning of FS 19 is about half a mile north of the intersection of WV 28/55, which is traversed by Scenic Route 13. Look for the Forest Service information board and map; you may want to stop and study it to get oriented. Behind the sign are outcroppings of nearly vertical beds of sandstone.

Ascending the Allegheny Front

Go west on FS 19. Almost immediately, the gravel road starts the ascent up the **Allegheny Front.** Maples, dogwood, and other hardwood trees dominate the forest. As you gain altitude, occasional views appear through the trees. As you pass the ridge at Fore Knobs, a level pasture opens up. Notice the rock outcroppings are no longer vertical but gently slanted to the west. At the top, the rocks will lie almost horizontally. Notice also that pines and other conifers are beginning to join the hardwood mix.

Finally, at the intersection with FS 75, you reach the top of the Allegheny Front, the edge of the Allegheny Plateau, and the edge of the Dolly Sods. Turn right on FS 75, which leads in 7 miles to Bear Rocks. (FS 19 goes straight; you will return here later and continue west on FS 19.) Along the way you'll pass several scenic turnouts, trailheads, and the Red Creek Campground.

The area was named for a Hessian German settler, John Dahle. He was a Hessian soldier who served with the British army against the colonists until he deserted. Dahle disappeared into the forests of the Allegheny Plateau and settled near here. The German's neighbors began to call him John Dolly. Dolly married and lived in the area until his death in 1847. His descendants grazed cattle and sheep in patches of high bluegrass called "sods" before they moved on to places where life was easier than on this windy mountain. As railroads flourished in the 1880s, the demand for lumber and wood products led to the widespread cutting of virgin forests throughout the state. The Dolly Sods was no exception, and the huge red spruce and hemlock—some up to 12 feet in diameter—that covered much of the upland succumbed to the saw and ax. The thick humus layer, no longer protected by the forest, quickly dried out and was burned off.

Congress established the Monongahela National Forest in 1920. Despite reforesting efforts by the forest service and the Civilian Conservation Corps, the region languished for years, virtually unknown and rarely visited. During World War II the land was used for target practice as the military hurled thousands of mortar shells onto the barren rocks and heath. Some unexploded mortar shells may still be found in remote areas, despite massive cleanups. These shells are dangerous. If you see one, do not touch it; report it to the US Forest Service district ranger in Petersburg.

One-sided spruce struggle to survive against the wind at Dolly Sods.
West Virginia Department of Commerce, Stephen Shaluta

For 7 miles FS 75 heads north along the top of the 4,000-foot-high plateau. Soon you are driving through nearly treeless heath amid white boulders of sandstone. The route offers numerous great places to catch a view. To the east (right), over the Allegheny Front, are spectacular views of the folded rocks of the Valley and Ridge province. On clear days you can see several distinct ridges lined up like giant waves; on especially clear days you may see the Shenandoah Mountain on the Virginia border, some 30 miles away.

The flat-lying rocks provide a broad, open plateau about 2,500 feet above the valley. The wind is almost constant, sweeping in from the west. Its murmur drones perpetually in the background. With no significant rises between here and the Rocky Mountains, the wind has more than a thousand miles to gain strength, and the jet stream often dips down from the stratosphere to howl over this high country. Ferocious storms, dense fog, heavy rain or snow, and a sharply dropping thermometer can materialize in a matter of minutes. The harsh climate is more like northern Canada than most of the US, and the plants that grow here are species adapted to endure those conditions.

The red spruce, stunted and lacking branches on the windward side, give testimony to the persistent wind. These one-sided sentinels reliably point east, a compass on the ridge tops. The plant life, surprisingly diverse, abundant, and colorful azaleas, mountain laurel, and rhododendron bloom in succession in spring. Summer brings abundant blueberries, huckleberries, and wild cranberries for the picking. Berries are also favorite foods of West Virginia's state animal, the black bear, who can occasionally be glimpsed up here, so make lots of noise and back slowly away if you see one. Don't turn and run, as that action labels you as prey. Red and gray foxes and bobcats have also been seen here, as well as rattlesnakes and copperheads, who hide under the rocks.

As the days cool in autumn, the berry leaves blaze in hues of bright red and orange against the dark green background of the spruce and pines.

The carnivorous insect-eating sundew plant and other vegetation of the heath can be seen from the boardwalk that runs through the bog on the Northland Loop Trail just before you reach the Red Creek Campground. Stay on the trail to avoid damage to this fragile ecological area. The campground offers 12 primitive campsites, pit toilets, and a picnic area.

The long ridge of the Allegheny Front is a major autumn bird migration route, and the Allegheny Front Migration Observatory, opposite the campground, has become a significant ornithological study area. Mid-September to mid-October is the prime time to see migrating flocks of broad-winged hawks. Thrushes, warblers, and other hawks are common. Don't worry if you are not an experienced birder; when the migration is in full swing there will be plenty of old-timers on hand eager to share their knowledge.

Several short trails lead to other scenic areas at the edge of the Allegheny Front. As you look down the Front, notice how quickly the lower slopes are dominated by hardwoods, protected from the harsh winds on the leeward side of the plateau. At Bear Rocks you'll see, well, bare rocks—huge blocks of white sandstone—plus more magnificent views.

The Dolly Sods Scenic Area—approximately 2,000 acres east of FS 75 from FS 19 to Bear Rocks, the area you have just driven through—was established in 1970 and is the most visited spot in this remote area. A few years later 10,215 acres to the west of FS 75 were designated as the **Dolly Sods Wilderness Area.** This undeveloped backcountry is traversed by rough, poorly marked trails intended for experienced hikers and campers. At lower elevations, the Dolly Sods Wilderness Area is covered with northern hardwood forests; at higher elevations, it's comprised mainly of red spruce and heath barrens. Some hikers say the area reminds them of eastern Alaska.

The backcountry also harbors creatures rarely found elsewhere in West Virginia such as bobcats, Cheat Mountain salamanders, and, at the most southern point in its habitat, the snowshoe hare. Deer, raccoons, woodchucks, skunks, and black bear are more common.

The most popular wilderness trail is the Red Creek Trail, which connects the north and south boundaries. This rocky and wet trail has a few short, steep sections. Because it fords Red Creek twice, it is not passable during high water. Do not attempt hiking here unless you are experienced, in good physical condition, and equipped for wilderness travel. Check in with the forest service.

The Ancient History of the Dolly Sods

The Dolly Sods evoke a sense of timelessness and wonder in many visitors like no place else in West Virginia. Despite the pillaging of its resources for several decades, today it seems to stand apart from the changing human world. Its white sandstone rocks were deposited more than 300 million years ago during Pennsylvanian time as a beach along the shoreline of the ancient Iapetus Ocean. The swampy land was repeatedly covered by shallow seas and lush marshes. The thick vegetation died and fell into the swampy water, piling up layer after layer to form peat. This was more than 100 million years before dinosaurs, mammals, and flowering plants appeared on Earth.

The beaches and peat were buried under other sediments, compacted, cemented, and finally transformed into sandstone and bituminous coal. Some 250 million years ago during ancient continental drift, what is now Africa began to slowly collide into North America from the east, forming the supercontinent known as Pangea. The resulting folding and faulting of the rocks east of the Allegheny Front raised towering mountains 20,000 to 30,000 feet above sea level.

Later North America and Africa separated into the present-day continents. About 60 million years ago, eastern North America was uplifted several thousand feet, and streams began to carve the old flat surface into the present hilly topography. In the folded Valley and Ridge province east of Dolly Sods, erosion-resistant sandstones formed the long mountain ridges so prominent today, as the softer limestones and shales eroded to make the valleys. Thousands of caves, some with miles of passageways, were dissolved out in the soluble limestones seen in the Virginias. The top of the Allegheny Front was raised higher than the ridgelines to the east; the Dolly Sods lie at one of the highest points. The Pottsville sandstone here is almost horizontal, giving the plateau-like surface.

A few thousand years ago—the blink of an eye in geologic time—glaciers to the north advanced to within a few hundred miles of West Virginia. The cool climate allowed growth of thick forests of spruce and other northern species; after the glaciers retreated and the climate warmed, the spruce forests continued to flourish on the high, windy ridge tops.

Humans created the last chapter in the formation of the Dolly Sods landscape. Since the 1880s we have cut down the huge virgin red spruce and hemlock forest, burned the thick undersoil so that the unceasing west winds could strip the remaining soil down to bare rock, and shot mortar shells over the land for military target practice.

Now you can stand on these timeless rocks amid the stunted, one-sided spruce and hear the winds whistling over the high plateau. As you gaze down on the sinuous ridges and valleys below, consider the changes the land has undergone: ancient shorelines, drifting continents and worn-down mountains, erosion, uplift, and logging. It has all combined to make the scene you see today, and it will be here long after you leave, always magnificent.

When you are ready to depart, retrace the 7 miles along the plateau on FS 75 to the intersection with FS 19. Turn west (right) on FS 19. This will take you to WV 32 about 1.5 miles from Canaan Valley State Park on the southern edge of Scenic Route 9.

Option: If you want to return to the starting point of this drive, do not turn around. Instead, continue north on FS 75 past Bear Rocks down the Allegheny Front 4.7 miles to WV 28-7. Turn south (right) on WV 28-7 and drive about 6 miles to the starting point at FS 19, or go another mile to the intersection of WV 28/55.

The main drive heads west, away from the Allegheny Front. Sheltered from the winds of the high plains, hardwood forests grow over the lower land. After about 1 mile you pass the Dolly Sods Picnic Area. Several trailheads on the left lead into the rugged bogs, cliffs, and plains of the Flat Rock and Roaring Plains. Only experienced hikers should attempt these trails, though they are better marked and experience somewhat less severe weather than those in the high wilderness section. They attract fewer hikers and may appeal to those who crave more solitude.

The drive heads down, down, down, but it is not as steep as the drive up the Allegheny Front. As you cross the boundary and leave the Monongahela National Forest, the road becomes paved, a few houses appear, and the route number changes to CR 45-4. A one-lane bridge at Red Creek provides access to the trout stream.

13

Potomac Highlands Loop

Seneca Rocks & Smoke Hole Canyon

General description: A 72-mile loop in the magnificent Potomac Highlands along mountain streams, past towering Seneca Rocks and through remote, foggy Smoke Hole Canyon.

Special attractions: Seneca Rocks, the Allegheny Front, tourist caves, and Smoke Hole Canyon.

Location: East-central West Virginia, between Petersburg and Franklin.

Driving route numbers: US 33, 220; WV 28, 55, CR 2, 2-3.

Travel season: Most parts of the drive can be made all year; the section through Smoke Hole Canyon may be closed in winter.

Camping: The US Forest Service maintains the 81-unit Seneca Shadows Campground near Seneca Rocks and the 46-unit Big Bend–Jess Judy Campground in Smoke Hole Canyon, with primitive facilities. Both are open from Apr through Nov, with some winter camping permitted. Two private campgrounds near Seneca Rocks are open all year with full facilities.

Services: There are no facilities in Smoke Hole Canyon. Gasoline, food, and lodging are available along other portions of the drive and in Petersburg and Franklin.

Nearby attractions: Dolly Sods and Spruce Knob.

The Route

The Potomac Highlands includes the headwaters of the two south branches of the Potomac River, moving through some of the Mountain State's most magnificent scenery adjacent to the imposing Allegheny Front east-facing escarpment. This 72-mile loop heads south along the North Fork (of the South Branch of the Potomac, but we'll call the western creek "North Fork" and the eastern one "South Branch" for short) past Seneca Rocks, one of West Virginia's best-known landmarks. Our route climbs over North Fork Mountain to go north along the South Branch through narrow Smoke Hole Canyon to complete the loop. Along the way are mountain vistas, imposing rock formations, and good fishing, camping, and hiking.

Most of the drive is on paved roads within the Spruce Knob–Seneca Rocks National Recreation Area, which in turn is part of the Monongahela National Forest. With many places of interest, the drive will take you all day, and you may want to plan on spending an extra day.

Two additional drives take you through the high country atop the Allegheny Front in the Spruce Knob–Seneca Rocks National Recreation Area. Dolly Sods (see Scenic Route 12) traverses the Arctic-like climate of the high plateau; Spruce Knob (see Scenic Route 14) climbs to the highest point in West Virginia.

Potomac Highlands Loop

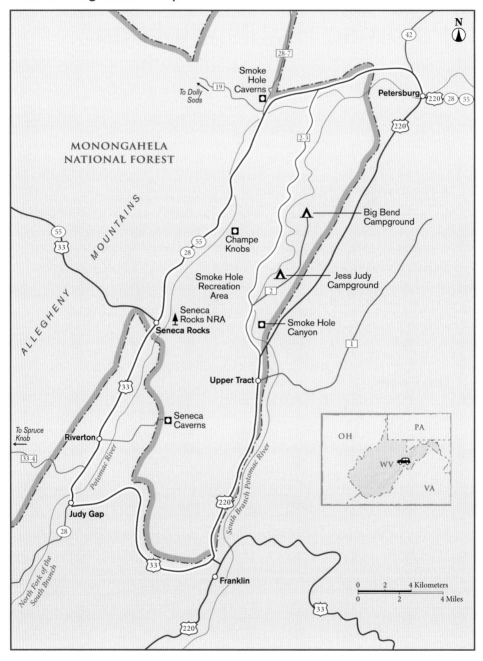

From Petersburg, drive west on WV 28/55 toward the imposing rock ridges of the Allegheny Front and Fore Knobs straight ahead. This route follows the North Fork through narrow North Fork Gap into the mountains and the Spruce Knob–Seneca Rocks National Recreation Area. Popular with anglers, the entire North Fork is usually well stocked with golden trout. Gentle rapids here make it particularly attractive to fly fishermen. The stream parallels the route for the next 30 miles, occasionally carving mini-caves in the rocks along its shores or sprawling out into a shallow bed littered with stepping stones.

Stay on WV 28/55. In about a mile, you'll see the entrance to **Smoke Hole Caverns** (smokehole.com), one of two commercially developed caves along the drive. Tunneling under New Creek Mountain, this cavern features what is called the "world's longest ribbon stalactite," as well as an underground trout pond and numerous flowstone formations that resemble frozen waterfalls. During the Civil War, soldiers stored ammunition in the cave; in later years moonshiners used the cold, pure waters of the North Fork to produce their potent beverage, hidden from prying eyes in the recesses of the cave. You'll see the coils and copper pot of an authentic still, minus the brew, standing close to Smoke Hole Caverns's entrance.

The imposing Allegheny Front rises 2,500 feet straight ahead on your route. The highest peaks in West Virginia are along this escarpment. The Allegheny Front marks the dividing line between the folded and faulted sedimentary rocks of the Valley and Ridge province to the east (left), which stretch like waves eastward into Virginia, and the flatter Allegheny Plateau to the west (right). The folding and faulting occurred over several tens of millions of years, beginning about 250 million years ago when the ancestral continents of Europe and Asia slowly heaved into North America.

Go left (south) on WV 28/55 at the intersection with CR 28-7. Drive 12, which begins about 0.5 mile to the right on CR 28-7, climbs up the Allegheny Front on dirt roads to the high country of the Dolly Sods. WV 28/55 winds through the deep valley of the North Fork River, rimmed here by North Fork Mountain on the east (left) and the escarpment of Fore Knobs and the Allegheny Front on the west. Soon you pass **Champe Knobs,** a near-vertical shaft of sandstone jutting several hundred feet into the sky.

Approaching Seneca Rocks

Champe Knobs is only a precursor to mammoth **Seneca Rocks** a few miles ahead. Look for its craggy top on the left around the bend in the road as you approach the intersection with US 33 and the entrance to the Seneca Rocks Discovery Center. An icon of West Virginia, this 900-foot-high behemoth of

Sandstone cliffs tower along the drive to Seneca Rocks.

sandstone was known to Native Americans and appeared on European settlers' earliest maps of the state.

The bare rock face, known as one of the most challenging climbs in the East, attracts climbers from around the country. If you want to try your hand at this, two nearby climbing schools will literally show you the ropes, even if you are a total beginner. You can also test your skills on the free beginner's climbing wall in the Discovery Center. If bare cliffs are not for you, you can still hike the steep West Side Trail 1.3 miles to an observation platform just below the ridgeline. This path is heavy on the stairsteps and switchbacks, but generous with trailside benches. At the top, you'll be rewarded with a stunning view of the valley—and you'll be able to look down on the swirling vultures. If you're a geocacher, take your GPS unit; there are several caches at the top of the trail as of this writing.

The **Sites Homestead** is located within walking distance of the Discovery Center. The first home built in the area by a European-American settler, the Jacob Sites home was originally constructed as a single-pin log home in 1839. The additions were constructed during Civil War times. Tours of the home are available on Saturday during the summer, and visitors can survey the heirloom gardens at any time during the regular day-use hours. Picnic sites are available here as well.

Seneca Rocks' first recorded climbers scaled its face in 1938. At the top they were surprised to find "D. B. Sept. 16, 1908" carved into the stone. Since then, climbers have developed dozens of routes up the rock face. During World War II, army mountaineer troops came here to train for action in the Alps.

Seneca Rocks challenges photographers as well. The west-facing rock is in shadow for most of the day. As the afternoon sun illuminates it, the rocks can shine a brilliant golden or soft yellow with dramatic hues and shadows. Early photographs and postcards show Seneca Rocks as having three humps. In 1987, the center piece, 20 tons of rock known as the Gendarme, suddenly collapsed, leaving Seneca Rocks with its current snaggletoothed appearance.

Both Champe Knobs and Seneca Rocks were formed in the nearly pure quartz of the Tuscarora sandstone, which has been folded here from its original horizontal position into a near-vertical orientation. The rock formations originally above and below the sandstone—softer shale and limestone—have been eroded away, leaving the imposing cliffs of sandstone.

Other trails lead through the thick woods to scenic overlooks on the ridge behind Seneca Rocks. Ask at the visitor center for information and maps. Exhibits at the visitor center give more details about the geology, plants, birds, crafts, and sometimes even music. Historic photographs let you compare the rock today with its 1987 precollapsed appearance. The visitor center is open Wednesday through Sunday from April through late October.

Next door is the Seneca Shadows Campground, run by the US Forest Service, and 2 private campgrounds are nearby. **Harper's Old Country Store** (harpersold countrystore.com), a true general store managed by the same family since 1902, is worth at stop at the intersection of US 33.

From Seneca Rocks continue south (left) on WV 28, now joined by US 33. At Riverton, a side trip leads right (east) on CR 9 through a cleft in the Tuscarora sandstone into Germany Valley for about 4 miles to **Seneca Caverns** (seneca caverns.com), the other commercial cave along the drive. The tour through Seneca Caverns is 0.75 mile through several large rooms. Because it's not on a main highway, Seneca Caverns has a little wilder feeling than caverns on the beaten path. Much of its flowstone is creamy white and sparkles with embedded calcite crystals. These commercial caverns are part of a cavern district. Much of the fertile farmland of Germany Valley is underlain by cavernous limestone, and a number of private wild caves attract spelunkers to this part of Pendleton County. Hell Hole and Schoolhouse caves, both for experts only, are known for their deep pits and sheer drops. Many caving techniques using ropes and mountaineering equipment were first developed in these caves.

Look for a large, arrowhead-shaped monument marking the site of Fort Hinkle, constructed by the mostly German settlers in 1762 to ward off Indian attacks. Later, during the Civil War, this area experienced some conflict as federal sympathizers from Seneca Rocks raided the strongly Confederate valley. Two

Climbers come from across the nation to scale Seneca Rocks.

miles past Riverton on the right at WV 33-4, Briery Gap Road, is the beginning of Scenic Route 14. That drive climbs on gravel roads to Spruce Knob, at 4,863 feet the highest point in West Virginia, and then goes to Spruce Knob Lake, a secluded mountain fishing pond for trout and smallmouth bass.

A mile past Riverton, at Judy Gap, turn south (left) on US 33. WV 28 goes straight. The drive climbs up and over North Fork Mountain, with scenic views of Germany Valley from the top of the ridge. The 24-mile North Fork Mountain Trail leads north along the ridgeline, passing some of the best views in the state on its way to the 4,300-ft. summit of Pike Knob. On the highway, it's a gradual descent to the intersection with US 220 about 13 miles from Judy Gap. Turn north (left) on US 220, which follows the South Branch of the Potomac River, here little more than a stream. (If you're hungry or need gasoline, the town of Franklin is about 1 mile ahead on US 220 South.) The countryside is more open and less rugged, with pastureland and numerous farms. The southern boundary of the Monongahela National Forest lies just to the west (left) of the highway.

Through Smoke Hole Canyon

About 12 miles from the intersection, past the little town of Upper Tract, turn left on CR 2 at the US Forest Service sign for **Smoke Hole Canyon.** The South Branch flows through a narrow gap that separates North Fork Mountain from Cave Mountain. Cliffs and steep slopes rise 800 to 1,000 feet high on both sides. In several places there is barely room for the road and river.

Swift rapids at Eagle Rock (named not for the bird but for the 1700s settler William Eagle), a vertical picturesque pinnacle of sandstone, make the river popular with bass and trout fishermen. Some say that Smoke Hole Canyon received its name because of the mist that often fills the valley; others claim that it is named for the smoke that issued from moonshiners' stills. Revenuers often disappeared there, and it was considered a dangerous place. The Nature Conservancy considers Smoke Hole Canyon to be one of the most biologically rich spots in the East and included it in its "Last Great Places" campaign. You soon pass the historical marker for Smoke Hole Cave (which is not the same as the commercial Smoke Hole Caverns) by the side of the road. This wild cave tapers to a natural chimney and has smoke stains on its ceiling, indicating that the Indians may have used it as a place for curing meat. It is on private property and not open to the public.

About 8 miles from US 220 is an intersection at a little country store. Follow the north (right-hand) branch (CR 2) a few miles along the river past the picnic area to the Jess Judy and Big Bend Campgrounds at the end of CR 2. On summer weekends you'll see numerous campers, trailers, and fishermen along this stretch.

The old Sites Homestead has been restored in the picnic area of Seneca Rocks.

Backtrack to the intersection at the store and turn north (right) uphill on CR 2-3. The road leaves the canyon and climbs into the high country where herds of sheep and cattle graze. Until a few years ago, this road was gravel and rough; recent rebuilding and paving have made travel easier. The route number changes to CR 28-3 as you cross the county line.

As you approach North Fork Gap, you'll see talus-covered slopes on the mountains ahead. The drive ends past the bridge of the South Fork at the intersection with WV 28/55, near where you began. Turn right (east) to go to Petersburg; turn left (west) to go to Smoke Hole Caverns and Seneca Rocks.

14

Spruce Knob & Spruce Knob Lake

West Virginia's High Point

General description: A 42-mile, winding drive up the steep Allegheny Front to the observation tower at Spruce Knob, West Virginia's highest point at 4,863 feet. From there, the drive descends to isolated Spruce Knob Lake and then passes along a small fishing creek. Almost the entire drive is on gravel roads.

Special attractions: Spruce Knob, alpine vegetation, superb views, and Spruce Knob Lake.

Location: East-central West Virginia, west of Franklin.

Driving route numbers: CR 29, 33-4; FS 1, 104, 112.

Travel season: Late spring through Oct. The road is not maintained in winter.

Camping: Spruce Knob Lake has 42 campsites but no facilities. Nearby is the equally primitive Gatewood Group Campground. Seneca Shadows at Seneca Rocks has 81 campsites with all facilities.

Services: None along the drive. The closest gas is in Riverton.

Nearby attractions: Seneca Rocks and Seneca Caverns and the Dolly Sods.

The Route

This 42-mile drive climbs up the 2,500-foot Allegheny Front on gravel roads to the alpine summit of Spruce Knob, the highest point in West Virginia. After a stop at the observation tower, the drive descends to isolated Spruce Knob Lake, then ends about midway between Elkins and Seneca Rocks on US 33/WV 55. The drive has sections that are steep and as twisty as a wounded copperhead. Most of this drive is over gravel roads. It is not suitable for trailers but can be driven in most passenger vehicles without four-wheel drive. The drive is not passable in winter, and extreme caution should be used any time of the year. Fog, storms, and snow are possible year round.

The drive to Spruce Knob begins at Briery Gap Road, CR 33-4, between Judy Gap and Riverton on US 33/WV 28. Look for the brown US Forest Service sign. The paved but narrow two-lane road leads immediately uphill through predominantly hardwood forests of maple, beech, and oak. Nearly vertical outcroppings of limestone and sandstone make testimony to the mountain-building forces that folded and faulted the rocks millions of years ago.

Bear left at the intersection (follow the signs). The pavement ends as you cross into the Monongahela National Forest and the Spruce Knob–Seneca Rocks

Spruce Knob & Spruce Knob Lake

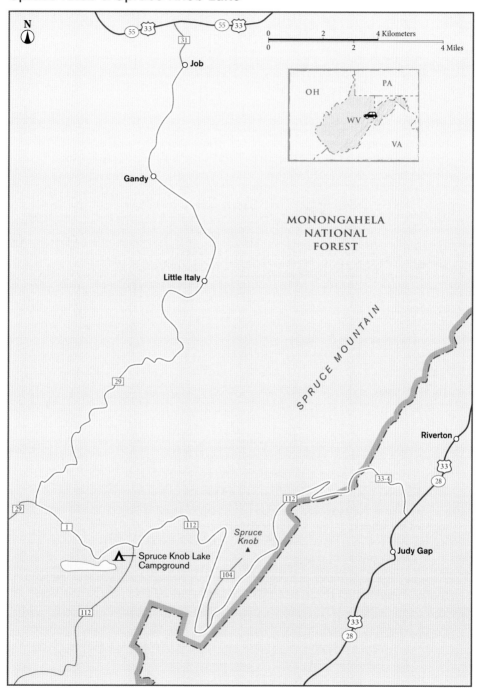

Spruce Knob is West Virginia's highest point at 4,863 feet.
WEST VIRGINIA DEPARTMENT OF COMMERCE, STEPHEN SHALUTA

National Recreation Area, and the route number changes to FS 112. The gravel road continues to ascend the long ridge of the Allegheny Front with numerous curves and turns. The hardwood trees become less numerous, giving way to mountain ash, red spruce, and low shrubs that can better withstand the more severe climate at this elevation.

After 10 miles of uphill work, you reach the intersection with FS 104 at the top of the ridge, about 2,500 feet above the valley. Turn right on this paved road along an open plateau mostly covered with slabs of sandstone. In about 2 miles, after passing a picnic area, radio tower, and several scenic views, the road ends at the Spruce Knob summit parking area. Chances are that a cold wind will be blowing steadily from the west; it usually is.

West Virginia's Highest Point

From here, a 5-minute walk over the rocky ground leads you to the observation tower. At an elevation of 4,863 feet, **Spruce Knob** is the highest point in West Virginia. There's no true summit here, just a hump slightly higher than the surrounding terrain, but the view from the 2-story tower is truly magnificent.

To the east and south ridge after ridge stretches in waves extending to the horizon. These are the folded rocks of the Valley and Ridge province; on clear days you may see 30 miles to the Shenandoah Mountain at the border of Virginia.

In other directions, the view of the Allegheny Plateau is somewhat less spectacular but no less interesting. The flat-lying rocks of this dissected plateau form a maze of irregular hills and valleys. The closer hills lie within the Monongahela National Forest.

The Allegheny Front extends as an irregular northeast–southwest ridge through much of eastern West Virginia and marks the transition between the Valley and Ridge province and the Allegheny Plateau. The apex of this ridge, much of it more than 4,000 feet above sea level, has a climate more like parts of northern Canada. The Dolly Sods (see Scenic Route 12) lie along this ridge, 25 miles to the northeast.

Adding to the severity of the weather is the constant whine of the wind, blowing perpetually from the west, unfettered in its sweep over this end of the continent. Fog and storms arise quickly, even in summer, and the weather can turn from sunny to snowy in minutes. So strong and so constant is the wind that the western branches of exposed red spruce never develop, and the one-armed trees point eastward as surely as a compass points north.

The rocks here lie flat and horizontal, huge slabs of Tuscarora sandstone undisturbed by the ancient folding and faulting to the east. Walk the 0.5-mile Whispering Spruce Trail with its outstanding views. Harsh the climate may be, but in the spring, in protected places between the red spruce, you'll see lady's slippers, mountain laurel, and azaleas blossom, followed in a few weeks by delicious huckleberries and blueberries. The forest service is fine with your picking them.

The Monongahela National Forest was established in 1920, but it wasn't until 1965 that the Spruce Knob–Seneca Rocks National Recreation Area was created, the first such designation in the country. These recreation areas are developed for public use.

All things must eventually end. To depart, retrace the drive on FS 104 to the junction with FS 112 and turn right (north). (If you've seen enough, turn left and go back to the starting point.) The pavement ends, and you soon head downhill. Watch for the first hardwood trees as you descend. Several trailheads lead off the road.

Spruce Knob Lake

Keep left at FS 1. The road to the right leads to the Gatewood Group Campground. After a few more miles, you pass the 42-site Spruce Knob Lake Campground. The lake itself is about 21 miles from the start. The 25-acre forest lake is a favorite spot for fishermen seeking bluegills and trout, and includes a wheelchair-accessible fishing pier. A 1-mile boardwalk circles the lake. To maintain the lake's pristine condition, the forest service doesn't allow gasoline-powered boats on its waters. Only crafts with small electric motors, canoes, and rowboats are permitted. Swimming is also forbidden.

Goldenrod blooms on the lower slopes of Spruce Knob.

Back on the road, you will turn right (north) in a few miles, at the stop sign on Rich Mountain Road, CR 29. This nearly level road follows Gandy Creek past fishing camps and picnic areas. A few wilderness campsites are scattered along the road. At mile 32, just as you're getting really tired of the dirt surface, you hit pavement.

The road leaves the national forest. After a few miles you pass the first group of houses, called Little Italy because of the nationality of its first settlers. The Spring Ridge and Huckleberry Trails lead from near this hamlet back up into the high country.

From here, it's a few more miles past several small communities to Job and the intersection with US 33/WV 55. The drive ends here. Turn left (west) to go to Elkins; turn right (east) to go to Seneca Rocks.

15

Highland Scenic Byway

High Peaks, Bogs & Waterfalls

General description: A 45-mile drive along the Highland Scenic Byway. It first traverses narrow hardwood valleys in Monongahela National Forest, passing by a unique bog and several waterfalls, and climbs into the high peaks of the Allegheny Mountains for unsurpassed views.

Special attractions: Cranberry Glades Botanical Area; sweeping vistas; the Falls of Hills Creek; and fishing, hiking, and camping.

Location: Central West Virginia between Richland and Marlinton.

Driving route numbers: WV 39/55,150; CR 39-5; FS 76, 86, 102.

Travel season: WV 39/55 is open all year; WV 150 is closed from Dec through

mid-Mar. Favorite times to visit are spring, for the wildflowers, and autumn, for the leaf color. Traffic is usually light.

Camping: The US Forest Service maintains Summit Lake and several smaller campgrounds along the drive, open from mid-Mar to Nov. Backcountry camping is permitted in several areas.

Services: All services are available at both ends of the drive in Richwood and in nearby Marlinton.

Nearby attractions: Cass Scenic Railroad and Snowshoe resort (see Scenic Route 17), Greenbrier River Trail, Beartown State Park, Droop Mountain Battlefield State Park, and Watoga State Park (all along Scenic Route 18).

The Route

For 45 miles the paved **Highland Scenic Byway** (byways.org) winds past wooded stream valleys, high country bogs, and mountain vistas. The first half of the drive begins in Richwood and follows WV 39/55 east through hardwood forests with side trips to waterfalls and the unique cranberry bog area. This section ends at Cranberry Visitor Center. The remainder of the drive is maintained as a parkway by the US Forest Service. It leads north and east on WV 150 past 4,000-foot peaks of the Allegheny Mountains to end at US 219.

More than 150 miles of hiking trails, from short, wheelchair-accessible boardwalks to strenuous backcountry treks, lead off from the route. Fishing, boating, hunting, and sightseeing are major activities.

The entire drive lies within the Monongahela National Forest and was designated as a National Forest Scenic Byway in 1989. It is one of three West Virginia highways that have been designated as a National Scenic Byway by the US Secretary of Transportation; the others are the George Washington Heritage Trail (see Scenic Route 7) and the Coal Heritage Trail (see Scenic Route 23).

The town of **Richwood** (cityofrichwoodwv.org) on the Cherry River lies at the western end of the drive, surrounded by the Monongahela National Forest.

Highland Scenic Byway

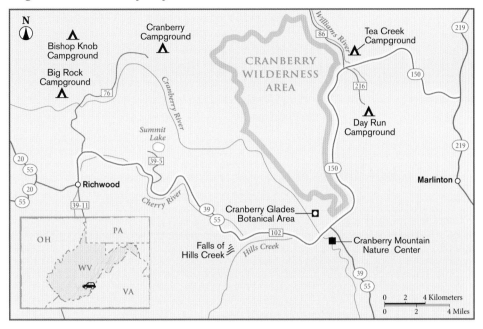

The town, originally named Cherry Tree Bottoms, was a lumber and mill town in the early 1900s. Much of that wood was processed into clothespins by Richwood's Dodge factory, the world's first and largest clothespin manufacturer.

Timber is still important today, but the town is better known as a gateway to recreational activities in the Monongahela National Forest. Richwood is the southern trailhead for the **Cranberry Tri-River Trail** (wvrtc.org), which follows a former railroad bed past woods, over trestles, and through tunnels for 16.5 miles. The trail is named for the rivers it meanders along—the Cherry, Gauley, and Cranberry.

Each April since 1937, Richwood has been host to the annual Feast of the Ramson. This festival honors the wild leek or ramp, *Allium tricoccum,* which grows abundantly in springtime in the surrounding hills and woods. Its bulbous, strongly aromatic root is savored by many, despite the lingering odor. You can fry ramps with potatoes, ham, or eggs, stuff them, serve them in soups or salads—but the true connoisseurs eat them raw.

From Richwood drive east on WV 39/55. Just outside of town a side road, FS 76, winds north (left) along the Cranberry River, a prime trout fishing stream. FS 76 leads 5 miles to a picnic area and the Big Rock Campground with 5 sites, and after another 6 miles, to the Cranberry Campground with 30 sites. The fishing sites here are usually less crowded than sites closer to the main highway.

The drive enters the designated Scenic Byway at the Gauley Ranger Station, and then passes through thick forests of beech, maple, oak, poplar, hemlock, and red spruce. About 8 miles from Richwood, just past the North Bend Picnic Area, another side road, CR 39-5, leads after 2 miles to **Summit Lake** and the Summit Lake Campground with 33 sites. The 42-acre lake, cherished by trout and bass fishermen, has a boat ramp and a wheelchair-accessible fishing pier. An easy 1.5-mile footpath with views of the lake begins here, as do several strenuous hikes into the national forest.

The Falls of Hills Creek

Back on the main drive, you'll reach the turnoff for the **Falls of Hills Creek Scenic Area** about 16 miles from Richwood. The three sparkling waterfalls plummeting over shale-limestone cliffs are not to be missed. Practically a drive-in waterfall, the first, 25 feet high, can be reached by a paved, 0.25-mile, wheelchair-accessible trail that has several steep grades. An unpaved and steeper trail continues downhill along a rhododendron-lined path less than a mile to two more falls. The first, a much wider falls, plunges 45 feet to the rocks below. The second, at 63 feet, is the second tallest waterfall in the state. Observation platforms at each falls give you unobstructed views of the cascading water. The best light for good photographs here occurs between noon and 2 p.m. The drive continues over a pass into a high bowl-like valley. Turn left (north) on FS 102 and drive 1.5 miles to the parking area and boardwalk in the 750-acre **Cranberry Glades Botanical Area,** a national natural landmark. (Before visiting the botanical area, you may want to proceed to the Cranberry Mountain Nature Center, 1 mile ahead on WV 39/55, for information and maps.) At an elevation of 3,400 feet, the tundra-like bowl holds several bogs that contain a relic population of plants more commonly found in northern Canada. These plants, including several varieties of orchids, the carnivorous sundew, monkshood, jack-in-the-pulpit, and skunk cabbage, flourished over large areas of West Virginia several thousand years ago when glaciers lay to the north. Now they are found in only a few high mountain areas of the state.

Bogs in the Wilderness

The bogs lie on the edge of 26,000 acres of backcountry called the **Cranberry Wilderness Area**. Locally known as the "glades," the bogs consist of spongy peat (partially decayed plant material) covered by sphagnum moss. A wheelchair-accessible boardwalk leads 0.5 mile through the bogs and the surrounding forest

The pristine Falls of Hills Creek are among the tallest waterfalls in the state.
WEST VIRGINIA DEPARTMENT OF COMMERCE, STEPHEN SHALUTA

of red spruce, hemlock, and yellow birch. Stay on the boardwalk to protect this fragile area.

The boardwalk is open 24 hours a day. Early morning is the best time to see birds, including the northern water thrush, here at the southern limit of its range. Forest service rangers conduct bog nature walks on weekend afternoons during the summer months. Check at the Cranberry Mountain Nature Center (next stop) for details.

You can drive another mile north on FS 102 to a barrier at the edge of the wilderness area. The road continues as a hiking trail with access to an extensive trail network. A favorite is the Cow Pasture Trail, a 6-mile loop through the wilderness with views of numerous beaver ponds and alder thickets.

Turn around, return to WV 39/55, and turn left (east). The **Cranberry Mountain Nature Center** is about 1 mile down the road, at the junction of WV 39/55 and WV 150, about 23 miles from Richwood. The center, open Thursday through Monday from May through October, provides displays, maps, hiking and camping information, and interpretive programs about the area. Ask here about guided tours of the Cranberry Glades Botanical Area and special programs. There are usually temporary exhibits of small animals such as turtles, snakes, and insects, which are returned to the wild after a week or two.

From the nature center, turn left (north) on WV 150, the West Virginia Scenic Highway. This is the beginning of the spectacular highland section of the drive, a 22-mile parkway that is the highest major road in West Virginia. The US Forest Service manages the road through the Allegheny Mountains for its scenic and recreational use.

Commercial vehicles are banned at all times. The road is not maintained in winter and is usually closed by snow from early December through March. The 45-mile-an-hour speed limit allows you to enjoy distant vistas, but stop for longer viewing. Numerous overlooks give you scenic views in all directions; all of them are equipped with wheelchair-accessible picnic shelters and restrooms. This wide, two-lane paved highway, in contrast to many other West Virginia mountain roads, has a minimum of curves and steep grades and is negotiable by all but the largest RVs.

On Top of the Byway

More than 60 percent of the parkway is above 4,000 feet, and a whopping 88 percent is above 3,500 feet. The scenic highway traverses the eastern boundary of the Cranberry Wilderness Area, with more than 70 miles of hiking trails leading off into the backcountry.

The author discovers a patch of ramps, wild shallots prized as a tonic in spring.

Wild asters along the Highland Scenic Highway.

As the road climbs to follow the crest of Black Mountain, the hardwood forests give way to red spruce and stunted scrub forest. Ridge tops are capped by a line of dark green spruce needles; the lighter green leaves of deciduous trees predominate at lower elevations. Several overlooks provide views into the Cranberry Glades and the Williams River Valley.

The road then dips down into the 3,000-foot-high river valley to cross the Williams River and FS 86 about 14 miles from the nature center. The **Williams River** is stocked with brown, rainbow, and brook trout; as you may guess, this makes it a popular fishing stream. FS 86 leads north about 1 mile to the Tea Creek Campground, with 20 sites, and south 4 miles to the Day Run Campground, with 12 sites.

After a gradual climb up Tea Creek Mountain, the road follows the high skyline for the rest of the drive, with almost constant views. At the Williams River Overlook, elevation 4,000 feet, you can look back at the river valley and look ahead to see the road as its sweeps over ridge after ridge. At other overlooks you may be able to see the extensive developments along the ridgeline to the east at the Snowshoe Mountain Resort and ski area.

The drive gradually descends to end at US 219 at an elevation of 3,525 feet, 7 miles north of Marlinton.

16

Railroad Loop & the Green Bank Observatory

Cass & Durbin Railroads

General description: A 30-mile drive through woods and fields of the Monongahela National Forest past two scenic railroads and the Green Bank Observatory. An optional return loop on a mountain road adds 16 miles.

Special attractions: Snowshoe Mountain Resort, Cass Scenic Railroad State Park, Greenbrier River Trail State Park, the Green Bank Observatory, and Durbin & Greenbrier Valley Railroad.

Location: East-central West Virginia, about 35 miles south of Elkins.

Driving route numbers: US 219, 250; CR 1; WV 28/92, 66.

Travel season: Late spring through Oct. The scenic railroads operate June through Oct on weekends and several weekdays; tours of the Green Bank Observatory follow a Thurs through Mon schedule from Memorial Day through Labor Day and run daily during the summer.

Camping: The Island Campground, in the Monongahela National Forest east of Durbin on WV 28, has 12 primitive campsites and is the only public campground near the drive. Near Cass, in Durbin, and north of Arbovale are several private campgrounds with all facilities.

Services: All services are available at Snowshoe. Reservations are recommended year-round and are a necessity during the ski season. Gasoline and food are available in all towns along the drive, with overnight facilities in Cass and other sites along the route.

Nearby attractions: Gaudineer Scenic Area, Greenbrier River Trail, Elk River Touring Center, and Cheat Mountain Salamander Scenic Railroad.

The Route

All aboard! Smell that coal smoke; hear the steam escaping. Look out for deer along the tracks. West Virginia has three scenic train operations, and this drive takes you by two of them.

One is located at the long-established Cass Scenic Railroad State Park. This train, powered by a restored logging steam locomotive, zigzags through switchbacks to Bald Knob, the top of Back Allegheny Mountain and third-highest peak in the state. Sometimes the engine pushes the train; other times it pulls. The other, privately owned Durbin & Greenbrier Valley Railroad, chugs along the banks of the secluded upper Greenbrier River, pulled by a small diesel. Both trains offer a variety of trips, including overnights in a caboose.

This driving tour also takes you to the mountaintop resort village of Snowshoe, with its array of ski lifts, trails, restaurants, condos, shops, and magnificent

Railroad Loop & the Green Bank Observatory

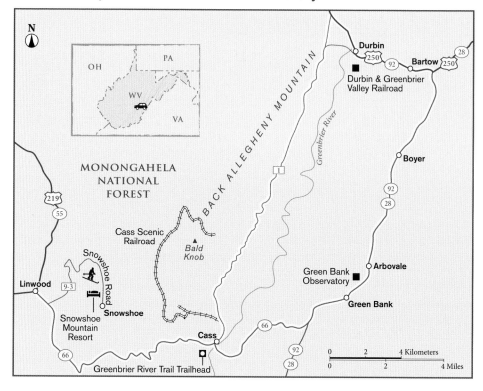

views. And if you'd rather ponder the far reaches of the universe, stop in Green Bank at the radio astronomy observatory (NRAO) where, in an isolated valley, radio telescopes scan the universe for signals from outer space.

The drive begins at the intersection of WV 66 and US 219/WV 55 about 2 miles from the entrance to **Snowshoe Mountain Resort** (snowshoemtn.com) and 12 miles west of Cass. Take a quick trip up the mountain for a glimpse of all Snowshoe Resort has to offer—everything from skiing, mountain biking, and sporting clays to, yes, snowshoeing—then grab a cup of fresh brewed coffee— there's even a Starbucks here—and head off on WV 66 to Cass and the scenic railroad. From Cass, continue east on WV 66 to the intersection with WV 28/92. Follow WV 28/92 for about 12 miles, stopping to visit the observatory and its interactive science center, then head to the intersection with US 250 and WV 92. From there, it is 4 miles to the Durbin excursion railroad and the end of the drive, for a total of about 30 miles. Most of the drive is through rolling country with gentle hills, past forests, fields, and small towns; all of it is over two-lane, paved primary highways, suitable for all vehicles. The entire drive lies within the boundaries of the Monongahela National Forest, but much of the land along the route is privately owned.

You can make this a loop drive by returning from Durbin to Cass on CR 1—better known as Back Mountain Road—a paved but narrow, steep, and winding road about halfway up Back Allegheny Mountain. Numerous scenic vistas are your payoff, but this 16-mile stretch is not recommended for trailers or for drivers who do not like mountain driving, and it will take you longer than retracing the drive along the state highways.

After a few miles you pass the entrance on the left to Snowshoe Mountain Resort, 2 miles uphill from WV 66. It's worth a trip, even if you do nothing else but look around to see the resort that has become West Virginia's newest village.

With 60 ski slopes and 14 lifts, Snowshoe has been known for years as a major destination for winter-sports enthusiasts. To keep its ridge-hugging lodges, shops, and restaurants busy and profitable during the rest of the year, the resort has added a golf course, more than 120 miles of mountain-biking trails, tennis, ATVs, paddleboarding, and hiking, plus cultural events from symphonies to Appalachian storytelling.

From Snowshoe to Cass

From Snowshoe, return to WV 66 and turn east (left). It's a 10-mile, mostly downhill drive through woods and fields to **Cass Scenic Railroad State Park** (cassrailroad.com), which encompasses most of the former logging village of Cass. The town's white company houses and sprawling company store appear much as they did around 1911 when Cass was a major timber center. Look for the depot beside the tracks, where you purchase tickets.

By 1900, when coal and lumber were West Virginia's major industries, a 3,000-mile network of railroad tracks spider-webbed the state. After World War II both the coal and lumber industries went into prolonged declines. The coal-powered steam engines were replaced by modern diesels, then sidelined as passenger vehicles when the public took to the highways in their new postwar cars on the growing interstate system. Much of the hauling, too, was taken over by trucks.

As smaller railroads were abandoned, rights-of-way became channels for hiking, biking, and equestrian trails. The **Greenbrier River Trail** (greenbrierrailtrailstatepark.com), one of the longest and most scenic in the country, has its northern trailhead in Cass. Hikers, bikers, and horseback riders can travel 78 miles along the rippling Greenbrier in this strip of a park to Caldwell, near Lewisburg, West Virginia (see Scenic Routes 18, 21, and 25).

At Cass, as at other logging centers, trees were cut down on the steep mountainsides, loaded onto logging trains, and hauled to the mill. Trains had to

A Shay locomotive pulls visitors up steep grades at Cass Scenic Railroad State Park.
WEST VIRGINIA DEPARTMENT OF COMMERCE, STEPHEN SHALUTA

negotiate steep grades and hairpin curves, which required locomotives built for power and maneuverability, with speed a distant secondary consideration. Don't be surprised if deer outrun the Cass train along the tracks.

Cass steam locomotives carry tourists in refurbished, open logging flatbeds as well as enclosed passenger cars. Steam locomotives, such as the 160-ton Shay, blow their shrill whistles and then huff, puff, and chug up the steep mountainsides. Several narrated train trips are offered. The longest takes 4.5 hours and climbs to the summit of Bald Knob, at 4,842 feet, with views over to the giant radio telescopes at Green Bank NRAO.

Trains run daily from Memorial Day through Labor Day and on weekends until late October, with special dinner trains, bluegrass rides, moonlight tours, and fall foliage trips. While waiting for your train, you can visit the historical district, the bustling Cass Country Store and the combined Historical Museum and Cass Showcase, filled with railroad and logging memorabilia.

Spotlight on Outer Space

Back in the car, continue east on WV 66 through the thick hardwood woodlands of the Monongahela National Forest. As you come out of the woods into open fields, look left. About 1 mile away, you'll see the dish of the world's largest radio telescope sticking out of the grounds of the Green Bank Observatory like a giant daisy.

Turn left (north) at the stop sign at the junction with WV 28/92. More satellite dishes and domes appear, and you head through the small and rather linear town of **Green Bank** to the entrance on the left to the observatory (greenbank observatory.org). This facility is one of the few observatories that analyze radio signals from space. Most telescopes look at the visible portion of the spectrum, the light waves that we see. The telescopes here study radio waves that emanate from the universe around us, from galaxies millions of light-years away and from other celestial objects such as pulsars and quasars.

The observatory, a facility of the National Science Foundation, was created in 1958 and sited in this remote valley to protect the sensitive receivers from human-made radio interference. The telescope you saw from the road began operation in late 1999 and was christened the Robert C. Byrd Green Bank Telescope in honor of West Virginia's late US senator. The GBT, as it is known, stands more than 480 feet high, with a reflector large enough to hold two side-by-side football fields. Its surface is adjustable to correct for minute changes caused by the temperature or the weight balance of the telescope. Scientists using it study the structure and chemistry of space and seek answers to what were formerly philosophical questions on nature of space time.

Several other telescopes are used in research here, including the world's largest equatorial mounted radio telescope, 140 feet high. Students gain experience on a 40-inch scope. Visitors tour the campus in special diesel buses; internal combustion vehicles interfere with radio signals. Guided tours are conducted daily in summer and Thursday through Monday in spring, fall, and winter. Fees are charged for the tours, but the visitors can explore the effects of signal interference from radio stations, manipulate a laser beam, and learn about NRAO scientists without charge, all in the Science Center. Special star viewings, films, and other programs are held throughout the year; check the website listed in the appendix for offerings.

An airstrip allows small aircraft to bring in some of the nearly 200 scientists from around the world who use the research facilities here each year. Some say that the town of Green Bank has the highest proportion of PhDs per capita in the country. Education has long been important here; a modest white cottage close beside the highway just south of NRAO has the reputed distinction of being the schoolhouse where Pearl Buck's West Virginia–born mother taught. The nearby birthplace of the Nobel Prize–winning author is included on Scenic Route 18.

When you leave the NRAO, turn left and continue north on WV 28/92. The drive continues along the level valley, paralleling Back Allegheny Mountain to the left. At the junction with US 250, look for the historic marker for the old **Travelers' Repose** house on the right. The home was the stagecoach stop favored by Confederate General Stonewall Jackson for its fresh venison and trout. The

original building was in the line of fire during the Civil War's Battle of Greenbrier River in October 1861, only to burn down after the war. The front of the house is original to the 1866 rebuilding. Confederate trenches are located about 3 miles up the small side road, CR 3, behind the house.

From Travelers' Repose, turn north (left) on US 250/WV 92 and drive about 4 miles to Durbin and the station for the Durbin Rocket excursion railroad.

The Durbin Rocket

The **Durbin Rocket** is one of four scenic railroads owned and operated by the **Durbin & Greenbrier Railroad** (mountainrailwv.com). The Durbin Rocket steam train is powered by a rare steam locomotive, Old No. 3, one of only three operating Climax-geared logging locomotives on earth. This 55-ton antique was built in 1910 for the Moore-Keppel Lumber Co. in nearby Randolph County. Today you can ride in authentic 1920-era coaches and vintage wooden cabooses behind No. 3 as she puffs and whistles her way along the upper reaches of the Greenbrier River for a 10-mile round trip. As at Cass, you can arrange to be dropped off in the caboose for an overnight in the quiet forest. Wildlife, including herons, waterfowl, and deer, is often abundant along this secluded river.

The railroad runs several trips daily during the warmer months and on weekends in spring and fall. The Durbin & Greenbrier Railroad operates three other scenic train trips: the Cheat Mountain Salamander, the Mountain Explorer dinner train, and the New Tygart Flyer, all of which leave from the Elkins station about 40 minutes north.

The main drive ends in Durbin. An optional return loop to Cass runs midline along the slope of Back Allegheny Mountain. This route is not recommended for trailers, large RVs, or drivers who do not like mountain driving. This 16-mile stretch is shorter than backtracking the way you came but will take longer.

To take this return loop, from Durbin go north on US 250/WV 92, which climbs up Back Allegheny Mountain. After about 1 mile turn left (south) on CR 1, Back Mountain Road, and follow the road back to Cass. The road is paved, but it is barely two lanes wide, hilly, and very curvy. Go slow; there are no signs warning you of curves. Most of the land along the route is used for grazing, with some scenic vistas and woods, but there are few houses and little flat ground. The optional loop ends in Cass by the railroad depot.

The Robert Byrd Green Bank Radio Telescope picks up distant murmurs from outer space.

17

New River Gorge & Bridge

Into & Out of the New River Gorge

General description: Twisting, switching back, and descending 1,000 feet from the canyon rim to the river, this 16-mile drive follows the old highway into the gorge of the New River, crosses the river, climbs up the other side of the gorge, and crosses the modern New River Gorge Bridge 876 feet above the river. It ends at the Canyon Rim Visitor Center of the New River Gorge National River. The drive is not suitable for RVs or large vehicles.

Special attractions: Challenging driving and spectacular views from above and below the bridge.

Location: South-central West Virginia near Fayetteville.

Driving route numbers: US 19; CR 82.

Travel season: All year, but snow may temporarily close the drive in winter. Traffic

is heaviest when fall colors are at their peak in late September and October and reaches a crescendo on Bridge Day weekend in the third weekend in October.

Camping: Public camping at nearby Babcock State Park, and at Pipestem and Bluestone State Parks a little farther away. More than half a dozen private campgrounds ring the gorge in the Fayetteville and Hico areas.

Services: All services are available in Fayetteville at the end of the drive, but no services are available along the drive itself.

Nearby attractions: Thurmond Depot (Scenic Route 19), Grandview State Park, Sandstone Falls, all part of the New River Gorge National River. Also nearby are the Beckley Exhibition Coal Mine, and Tamarack, West Virginia's arts and crafts exhibition and retail center.

The Route

Sometimes you just have to state the obvious—the 14-mile **New River Gorge** is an awesome place. Combine the stunning beauty of ash-gray cliffs rising hundreds of feet over pounding rapids with the man-made wonder of an 87-story steel-arch bridge spanning the gorge, and you have a not-to-be missed West Virginia sight for your bucket list. Held in awe by whitewater enthusiasts, the New River churns and tosses through this 1,000-foot-deep canyon in southern West Virginia, descending 750 feet in the 50 miles from Bluestone Dam in Hinton. (By comparison, the Mississippi falls just over twice that in its entire 2,300-mile journey.) The New River and the nearby Gauley boast some of the best whitewater in the country; they comprise two of the top three rafting rivers in the East.

Crossing this canyon once entailed an arduous 45-minute drive down winding roads in and out of the gorge. When the 3,030-foot-long **New River Gorge Bridge** opened in 1977, travel time was reduced to one minute. In 2005, the structure was further immortalized when its span was depicted on the new West Virginia state quarter.

New River Gorge & Bridge

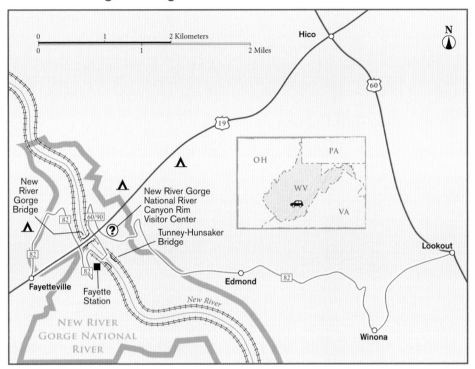

This drive follows the old road into the New River Gorge from the old coal town of Lookout on CR 82, a paved, but narrow, steep, and extremely curvy road. The climb up the other side is equally tortuous. At the top, near Fayetteville, the drive follows US 19 across the New River Gorge Bridge to the US Park Service's New River Gorge National River Canyon Rim Visitor Center. Although the drive is only 16 miles long, the curves and elevation change will make it seem twice that length.

This drive is not suitable for towed vehicles, RVs, and other large vehicles. If mountain roads make you queasy, skip this drive. CR 82 is a twisting roller-coaster ride, even by West Virginia standards. Whether or not you take the complete drive, you can still enjoy the drive over the bridge on US 19 and the views, exhibits, hikes, and other activities at the visitor center.

The drive starts at the town of Lookout, near mile 57 on US 60 at the intersection of US 60 and CR 82. Both Lookout and the next town, Winona, grew rapidly during the gorge's coal boom days from 1890s through the1920s; former department stores, pool halls, and lodges stand empty or repurposed into homes in towns one-fifth their former size. Go west on CR 82, heading downhill. At first the grades are easy, a warm-up for what lies ahead, and land is flat enough for agriculture. Turn right at the stop sign in Winona, still following CR 82.

At the tiny post office in Edmond, bear left. One of the smallest in the state, this facility can comfortably accommodate only two patrons. Edmond lies close to the edge of the gorge, and the grades steepen as you descend over the canyon lip.

Descending into the Gorge

After you cross into the national river boundary, the road descends precipitously with numerous sharp curves. CR 82 goes left at a fork bordering a small parking area for hikers and rock climbers. Beyond the fork, the road becomes one-way as it hugs a sheer cliff. (This is your last chance to bail out before the steepest and curviest part of the drive. If you've had enough, go right on the unnumbered road, which will eventually lead you to US 19 near the Canyon Rim Visitor Center.)

On CR 82, you'll encounter a constant barrage of hairpin curves, switchbacks, and steep downgrades—too many to depict on the map. This is a great motorcycling route, but don't underestimate some of these tight turns in a car. You'll see occasional pull-offs for folks who want to hike, rock climb, just take their eyes off the road to see the view of the river below. Look for signs of the many mining communities that used to border this gorge.

If this seems like a difficult trip, remember that before 1977, this was the only way to cross the river. You'll have numerous views of the river and the span, supports, and undersides of the New River Gorge Bridge as the drive crisscrosses underneath its span.

The rocks and cliffs of the gorge are sedimentary stones, deposited during the Mississippian and Pennsylvanian periods, 320 to 330 million years ago. The vertical cliffs are well-cemented long-lasting sandstone and conglomerate; the gentler slopes are made up of shale, siltstone, and thin beds of limestone. Rhododendron and mountain laurel grow in profusion on all but the sheerest of cliffs, and hardwood trees cover any level ground.

Most of the rocks were deposited as erosion sediment in shallow water or swamps; the sediment was probably worn away from a southeastern highland about where the Blue Ridge Mountains are located today.

The sheer cliffs, known to geologists as the Nuttall sandstone and to rock climbers as The Wall, extend for many miles along the gorge. About 1,400 rock-climbing routes have been established over these cliffs; many are described in the FalconGuide *Rock Climbing Virginia, West Virginia, and Maryland,* published by Globe Pequot Press. Most are for expert or advanced climbers and rated 5.9 or higher.

The New River is actually one of the world's oldest rivers.

Numerous coal seams run through the section, some of which are still being mined nearby. The coal beds formed from dead swamp plants whose fossil remains can often be seen in the coal. The most notable coal deposit is the Sewell seam, once widely known as the "Famous New River Smokeless Coal." It was rarely less than 4 feet thick and often sometimes 9 to 10 feet thick. Miners were especially fond of this high-grade coal seam, because its tall underground passages allowed them to walk upright. The ghost town of Sewell, once a thriving mining town, lies along the bottom of the gorge a few miles to the south.

When the Appalachian Mountains were uplifted and folded beginning 225 million years ago, the New River area rocks were tilted to the northwest. The gorge is about 1,600 feet at its deepest, and only a fraction of a complete cross section of this rock can be seen at any one spot.

After a final curve, the road reaches Fayette Station, little more than a narrow ledge of level land at the bottom of the V-shaped valley. The road, the railroad, and the river share the cramped flat space, with steep cliffs rising up on both sides. Like most of the former coal mining towns along the New River, little remains of the town of Fayette Station. The New River, about 100 yards wide here, looks fairly benign. But the sound of the rushing water is always in the background—a minor gurgle in low water and a thundering bellow when the river runs full. The famous, bone-rattling rapids are farther upstream.

Watch for trains as you cross the tracks; this is still an active main line of the CSX Corporation. Laying tracks along river valleys such as the New was a challenge, but it was cheaper and faster for the vital railroad link than blasting the tunnels and constructing bridges and trestles. Diesel engines have replaced the coal-driven locomotives, but freight trains, some hauling several hundred cars filled with coal, still snake their way through the canyon. Amtrak passenger trains, most equipped with scenic observation cars, provide sightseers with a close-up view of the federally protected river gorge.

You can pull over in one of several parking spots to admire the river scenery at your leisure. Many commercial raft trips end here. The takeout areas allow fishermen to try their luck at hooking prized smallmouth bass and walleyes.

How old is the New River? Its deep gorge and the fact that it flows completely across the Appalachian Mountains from east to west have often led to the claim that it is the second oldest river in the world after the Nile. But there is no accurate way of dating a river. The New must be younger than the enclosing rocks (320 million years). It must have formed after the Appalachian Mountains building phase (225 million years) and the Appalachian uplift (65 million years ago).

Studies of the erosion rates of major rivers of the US yield a figure of about 1 foot of erosion every 6,000 years; this indicates an age of about 10 million years to erode 1,600 feet at the deepest part of the gorge. Other comparison studies suggest it could be between two and three millions years old.

At the Bottom of the Gorge

Eventually you reach the narrow bridge across the New River at the bottom of the gorge, the small bridge that used to handle all traffic before the New River Gorge Bridge was built over the canyon. This low bridge, known as the Tunney-Hunsaker Bridge, was historically reconstructed in 1997. The bridge is named for Fayetteville's beloved police chief, a former boxer who took on heavyweight champ Muhammad Ali at the start of Ali's career in 1960. A water gauge is painted on a rock at the foot of the bridge, and rafter guides often consult it before embarking on their runs.

You can pull over at the parking area and walk across the bridge. The last major rapids of the New River Gorge lie several hundred feet upstream to the left, and with good timing, you may see rafts or kayaks as they traverse this final stretch of whitewater and pass under the bridge.

After crossing the bridge, the drive turns right. High in the distance are the spans of the New River Gorge Bridge. What goes down must eventually come up, and soon you begin the ascent out of the gorge. This side is every bit as steep and undulating as the descent, crossing under the arches of the New River Gorge Bridge several times. After leaving the gorge, you pass several rafting and rock-climbing outfitters.

CR 82 ends at the stop sign at the intersection with US 19 on the eastern edge of **Fayetteville.** Although you are only 14 miles from the start in Lookout, you may feel as if you've disappeared into a time pocket for the past half hour; it feels like much longer. Turn right (west) on US 19 to visit downtown Fayetteville, with

Fayetteville is named for Lafayette, friend to the American patriots during the Revolution.

its old redbrick stores, restaurants, and outdoor outfitters. The statue in front of the courthouse is Marquis de Lafayette, for whom the town was named, but who was unlikely to have visited the area when he fought for the patriot's cause in the American Revolution. Fayetteville's main industry is catering to the needs of the thousands of kayakers, rafters, rock climbers, hikers, and other outdoor-loving visitors. Some two dozen whitewater-rafting companies are located in town or nearby. (See the appendix for numbers for the West Virginia Division of Tourism and the Fayetteville Convention & Visitors Bureau. There are too many rafting companies to list individually.) Fayetteville's granola atmosphere is enhanced by a partially restored historic area and numerous restaurants that help satiate the gargantuan appetites whetted by an energetic day on the river.

Across the New River Gorge Bridge

After gazing at the underside of the New River Gorge Bridge during your long journey through the gorge, you should now be ready to drive over it. The bridge is about 1 mile east of Fayetteville on US 19.

If you want to walk over the bridge, come back on **Bridge Day,** the third Saturday in October, the one day of the year when the bridge highway is open to foot traffic. You will have to share the road with more than a quarter of a million other visitors who come to watch the rappellers and parachutists drop over the side. Music, food, crafts, and guided walks are part of the festivities. This gala affair, sponsored by the Fayette County Chamber of Commerce, has become West Virginia's largest festival.

You may also examine all the beams and bolts at close range by going under the bridge on a catwalk tour that travels in the structure just under the roadway. Offered collaboratively between the park service and the highway department, New River Gorge Bridge Walk offers daily catwalk walking tours for about $60–$90. The tours are 2 to 3 hours in length, and open to participants who are at least 10 years old and can walk 1.5 miles. Bridge walkers are fastened onto a safety cable at the beginning of the tour, making it impossible to fall from the bridge. The **Canyon Rim Visitor Center** (nps.gov/neri/planyourvisit/crvc.htm) is located just beyond the north end of the bridge. This visitor center, the largest in the park, contains a museum with exhibits on the history and natural features of the area. A wheelchair-accessible walkway leads to an observation deck at the edge of the gorge for views gorge; a boardwalk descends 100 feet into the gorge. Rangers are available for additional information and for conducted talks and tours. A variety of trails start here, ranging from an easy loop along the rim of the trail to an arduous round-trip trek to the bottom of the gorge and back.

Bridge Day, when folks parachute off New River Gorge Bridge, is West Virginia's biggest festival. WEST VIRGINIA DEPARTMENT OF COMMERCE, STEPHEN SHALUTA

18

Greenbrier River Valley

Lewisburg to Marlinton

General description: This 44-mile drive climbs small hills and one steep mountain along the free-flowing Greenbrier River, known for its outstanding hiking, canoeing, and fishing. The drive passes a major cavern, a Civil War battlefield, an intriguing rock formation, and the birthplace museum of author Pearl S. Buck, winner of both the Nobel and Pulitzer prizes.

Special attractions: Lost World Caverns, Smooth Ambler Spirits distillery, Greenbrier River Trail State Park, Beartown State Park, Pearl S. Buck Museum, and Droop Mountain Battlefield State Park, and Watoga State Park.

Location: Southeastern West Virginia, off I-64, exit 169, near White Sulphur Springs and 14 miles from the Virginia border.

Driving route numbers: US 219; WV 39/55.

Travel season: All year. Spring and fall are the most popular and most colorful travel times.

Camping: Watoga State Park has 2 campgrounds with 88 sites, most with hookups. The Greenbrier River Trail has several primitive campsites. There are private campgrounds at Lewisburg and Marlinton.

Services: All services in Lewisburg and Marlinton. Gas and food are available in Hillsboro and most of the small towns along the drive.

Nearby attractions: Organ Cave, Watoga State Park, Lewisburg's North House Museum, Lewisburg's Carnegie Hall, Cranberry Glades Botanical Area, Highland Scenic Drive, Cass Scenic Railroad, Greenbrier State Forest, and The Greenbrier resort in White Sulphur Springs.

The Route

At the beginning of the 20th century, the Greenbrier River Valley was a thriving lumbering area, as trains loaded with timber for the growing cities on the Eastern Seaboard chugged their way through the valley. Today the trains are gone, and the formerly bare hills are again covered with hardwood forests. The railroad is also gone; in its place is the Greenbrier River Trail State Park, a shoestring hiking and biking trail that winds along the river for 78 miles.

Parallel to the Greenbrier River, US 219 also winds northward. This drive follows US 219 and the Greenbrier Valley for 44 miles from Lewisburg to Marlinton. The valley, wide at Lewisburg, becomes narrower and more wooded as you head north.

Several outstanding natural and historical places lie along the drive, including the commercial Lost World Caverns, the Beartown State Park grottoes, the Civil War battlefield at Droop Mountain, Pearl S. Buck's birthplace museum, the wooded hills of Watoga State Park, and the historic town of Marlinton. Side trips will add another 10 miles or so to the mileage and extra time to the basic hour-long drive.

Greenbrier River Valley

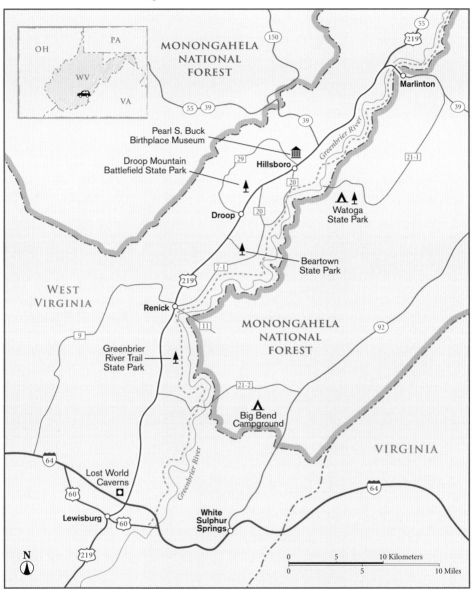

Our tour of the Greenbrier River Valley begins in **Lewisburg** at the junction of US 219 and US 60, just off I-64 exit 169. It connects in Lewisburg with Scenic Route 21, a 52-mile drive between Athens (near Princeton) and Lewisburg. The historic town of Lewisburg was established in 1782 and today features more than seventy 18th- and 19-century historic buildings, including Lewisburg's own Carnegie Hall and a church with a cannonball lodged in its side.

Before leaving the area, consider a visit to Lost World Caverns, a commercial cave known for its huge rooms, totem pole–like stalagmites, and sparkling calcite formations. To reach the cave go north from downtown on Court Street, which becomes Fairview Drive, and follow the signs to the cave for about 2 miles.

Exploring Lost World Caverns

When the **Lost World Caverns** (lostworldcaverns.com) were discovered in 1942, the only way in was a 120-foot rappel or rope-ladder descent through a grapevine-covered sinkhole. Known then as Grapevine Cave, it was visited only by the most skilled cavers for the next 29 years. When the cave was developed for the public in 1971, the owner drilled a sloping access tunnel, installed electric lighting, and built underground walkways past the magnificent stalactites, stalagmites, and other flowstone formations. Still, the self-guided tour consists of about 0.5 mile of almost constantly climbing up and down steps, and it may be too strenuous for some. But for those who can handle the exercise, this cavern offers many lovely cave formations within a small space.

The main room—the largest cave room open to the public east of Carlsbad Caverns—is more than 300 feet long and 50 feet wide, with a ceiling that arches more than 100 feet overhead. At one point you can look straight up 12 stories to a tiny pinpoint of light that marks the original natural entrance. The cave, a Registered National Landmark, is one of hundreds of caves tunneling through eastern West Virginia's karst topography.

If a lighted tour over boardwalk is too tame for you, ask about guided tours to some of the dark areas of the cave beyond the developed section. Walking the lighted paths of a commercial cavern may seem eerie, but wild caving through musty passageways seldom probed by cavers' lamps is an alien adventure. A layer of moist silt makes every surface seem rubbed in soap—great for slithering through tight spots but not so good for clambering uphill. You'll use all your breakfast calories and every muscle group climbing, crawling, twisting, jumping, and pulling yourself through the cave endurance course, but it's an adventure. This is where the bones of an extinct Pleistocene bear were discovered. Hardhats and headlamps are supplied

Before you leave, check out the museum—West Virginia's first little natural history museum. Lost World has a collection of replicas of the Smithsonian Institute's castings of dinosaur bones—an allosaurus, triceratops, a European cave bear, and much more. Six-year-olds especially like the polished, petrified dinosaur poop.

West Virginia's state theater graces Lewisburg's downtown.

When you're ready to begin the actual drive, go north on US 219 from Lewisburg, crossing under I-64. The Greenbrier Valley here is broad and open, dotted with farms, large herds of cattle, and verdant low hills.

Just north of Lewisburg, look for the sign for **Smooth Ambler Spirits distillery** (smoothambler.com) at the corner of US 219 and Airport Road on the right (east). The Greenbrier Valley's hard, limestone water makes good whiskey, and this artisan distillery located in Lewisburg's industrial park for that reason. The small-batch operation offers tours and tastings on Friday and Saturday afternoon—just follow Industrial Park Road a mile from its intersection with Airport Road to the red, barnlike building.

Paralleling US 219 a mile or two to the east (right) are the Greenbrier River and the **Greenbrier River Trail State Park** (wvstateparks.com/park/greenbrier-river-trail). The Greenbrier River Trail tags the river for 78 miles from Caldwell, east of Lewisburg, north to Cass. The packed dirt trail follows a former C&O railroad bed over 35 bridges and through two tunnels. The first trains, loaded with timber, puffed along the tracks here in 1900 but ended service in 1978.

The railroad donated the right-of-way to the state, with the provision that it be maintained in the slight possibility of future railroad use. Voted one of the 10 best and most beautiful rail trails in the country, the Greenbrier has gentle grades—less than 1 percent—favored by equestrians, novice bikers, and families with children. Fishing—the river is known for its trout and smallmouth bass—canoeing, and just floating on tubes down the clean Greenbrier River provide enjoyable respites from hiking and biking. Cross-country skiing is popular in winter.

The Greenbrier River Trail is accessible from several points along the drive; at side roads and intersections along US 219 look for signs directing you to the trail. You can check it out by turning right on WV 11 in Renick, about 10 miles from Lewisburg. The parking area and trail access lie within 0.5 mile of US 219, just before the bridge. If you visit in springtime, hike north on the trail for a mile or two to view trillium, redbud, and other wildflowers. Islands in the river form shallow feeding grounds for migratory fowl, such as wood ducks and Canada geese, making this section a choice destination for birders.

Most through hikers and bikers traverse the trail from north to south, following the slight downhill grade of the trail and the river. On foot the entire 78-mile trail can be covered in five or six days; astride a horse or bicycle, it takes two or three days.

After visiting the trail return to US 219 and turn north (right). As you drive north, the valley gradually narrows, and hardwood forests predominate over

The Droop Mountain Tunnel in Greenbrier Trail State Park makes for a cool respite on a hot day.

farmlands. A few minor hills, tame by West Virginia standards, add interest. About 21 miles from Lewisburg, just past the Pocahontas-Greenbrier County boundary, look for the sign on the right for Beartown State Park. (Use caution; this is an acute right turn.) Follow the side road to Beartown's parking lot.

Beartown's Nooks & Crannies

At 110 acres, **Beartown State Park** (wvstateparks.com/park/beartown-state-park) is one of the smallest parks in the state. But this meandering labyrinth of house-size boulders seems its own little world; an elf or troll would not be out of place. The rock, known as Droop or Pottsville sandstone, was originally deposited along the edge of ancient seas. During several thousand years of exposure on this Droop Mountain ridge, it has eroded, weathered, and split along vertical joints in the sandstone. The resulting multitude of fissures, many of them 30 to 50 feet deep, are wide enough to walk through. They are surrounded by towering mossy boulders.

The boardwalk leads 0.5 mile up, over, under, down, and around through this maze of rocks. A forest of hemlock, oak, and birches creates a thick canopy of leaves overhead, and ferns and mosses cover the forest floor and sprout from almost every tiny crack in the rock. Lichens grow where the ferns and mosses do not, forming gray blankets on the bare rock. Some elephant ear lichens are 5 feet across and more than 100 years old. It's almost always damp here, adding to the sense of primeval mystery and timelessness. Be forewarned: Many people who expect to spend half an hour are bewitched into staying half the day.

Bears are almost never seen at Beartown. But early settlers thought the huge boulders would be a good place for bears to live, and the name stuck. The gate to the parking area is locked from November through March. Because this is an extremely fragile ecological area, you must stay on the boardwalk. There is no fee.

The State's Last Civil War Conflict

To continue the drive, return to US 219, turn right (north) and proceed 4 miles to another great West Virginia state park, **Droop Mountain Battlefield State Park** (wvstateparks.com/park/droop-mountain-battlefield-state-park). If you hear shots on an October weekend, it's not your imagination (although several ghost hunters do swear the park is haunted); reenactments of the Civil War battle are held here every other year. One of West Virginia's largest, and its last significant, Civil War conflict was fought here on November 6, 1863. The decisive Union victory ended Confederate efforts to control the new state. Approximately 1,700 troops under Confederate General John Echols clashed with 3,800 Union soldiers under

View of Pocahontas County from Droop Mountain.

General William Averell, intent on destroying the Virginia & Tennessee Railroad to the southeast.

Confederate troops dug in at a pass over Droop Mountain. While the main federal force bombarded the Confederates, another blue-coated wing circled around to surprise the Confederates' left flank. Following nearly six hours of artillery fire, musketry, and hand-to-hand combat, Averell's infantry forced the Confederate troops into a wedge, and the retreat became a rout. Confederate troops retreated south into Virginia, and West Virginia remained under federal control.

The park superintendent can point out where big Austrian bullets marked the path of the 28th Ohio up the mountain from the north. He can also show you an oak tree beside the parking lot where he discovered federal bullets, one with toothmarks. The bitten bullet, now in the park museum, resembles a wad of well-chewed gum.

"Poor fellow probably had these other bullets removed right under this tree, without anesthesia," past park superintendent Mike Smith said. "That soldier literally bit the bullet. Only way to prevent infection was to amputate. His buddies would pop a lead bullet between his back teeth—it being malleable and not likely to break his molars—and hold him down for a rough few minutes."

The battle cost 600 men their lives; a few are still buried here. A museum behind the park headquarters contains artifacts and exhibits, including an account of the battle in the November 21, 1863, edition of the *New York Times*.

Whether you tour the battlefield or not, be sure to stop at the observation tower for views of the Greenbrier River Valley. Short hiking trails lead visitors past various battle lines and overlooks.

From Droop Mountain, continue north on US 219. After a few miles you reach the town of Hillsboro, where a former general store sells crafts and tasty sandwiches.

Just past town on the left is the restored **Pearl S. Buck Birthplace** (pearls buckbirthplace.com) museum of the famed author. The large house was built by her maternal great-grandparents, the Stultings, in the 1870s as a replica of the family home in Holland; many of the furnishings reflect the styles of that period.

Buck was the daughter of Presbyterian missionaries stationed in China, who returned home to the Stulting house for their daughter's birth in 1892. A few months after her birth, Pearl Comfort Sydenstricker returned to China with her parents, and, except for four years at Randolph-Macon Women's College in Virginia and a postgraduate year at Cornell University in New York, she spent the first 40 years of her life in China.

Buck wrote 85 books, including *The Good Earth,* for which she received the Pulitzer prize. In 1938 she was awarded a Nobel. Until her death in 1973, she continued to publish and was active in civil rights and women's rights groups. While most of her books deal with China, she wrote several biographical books that showed her strong affection and emotional ties to the hills of West Virginia.

Although she died more than 40 years ago, visitors to her birthplace can still buy unused, first-edition books autographed with Buck's crisp handwriting. The famous author set aside afternoons to autograph her books.

Scattered around the 12-room house museum are ingenious pieces of furniture created by her grandfather and books by Buck's younger sister, Grace Sydenstricker Yaukey. The smaller building to the left of the manor house is her father's boyhood home, the Sydenstricker House, moved in pieces from Greenbrier County. The Pearl S. Buck Birthplace is open Friday through Monday, from late May through October. An admission fee is charged. The birthplace celebrates Buck's birthday the last weekend in June, as well as an autumn Harvest Moon Festival.

Watoga, River of the Islands

A mile north of the Buck museum on US 219, a sign on the right directs you to **Watoga State Park** (watoga.com) on the opposite side of the Greenbrier, about 3 miles south on WV 27. At 10,100 acres, Watoga is the largest state park in West

Greenbrier County has a peaceful pastoral feel.

Virginia and is one of the most popular. Hiking, boating, camping, fishing, and swimming at the park lake are the main activities. In the Cherokee language, the park's name means "river of the islands," which aptly describes the numerous shallows, low islands, and sandbars along this stretch of the Greenbrier.

Two campgrounds provide 88 campsites, and there are 34 rental cabins. Numerous trails lead through the woods and the 400-acre arboretum. Several picnic areas provide attractive places to sup, particularly the T. M. Cheek Overlook atop one of the highest ridges in the park. If you like being served, try the park's restaurant at the lake. During the summer months rangers schedule a variety of nature walks, hikes, and other activities. Ask the rangers how to see the old bank vault that is all that remains of the logging town of Watoga along the Greenbrier River Trail.

Most of the park's facilities lie in the northern half of the park; the southern section, popular with wilderness hikers, borders undeveloped Calvin Price State Forest and the Monongahela National Forest. The park is open from April through December, with limited facilities accessible in winter.

From Watoga, the drive to **Marlinton** is 14 miles north on US 219. At the restored 1904 building that houses the **Pocahontas County Historical Museum** in Marlinton are many exhibits and photographs of Marlinton's rich history, including Indian artifacts, Civil War memorabilia, and railroad and timber industry displays, plus early farm equipment and domestic appliances. On the museum grounds is an 1840 log cabin.

The Greenbrier River and the Greenbrier River Trail run through Marlinton, the largest town in Pocahontas County, unless you count Snowshoe on President's Day weekend.

Marlinton is the end of this drive. The Greenbrier River Trail continues north about 25 miles to terminate in Cass (via US 219 and WV 1 by vehicle). Cass is near the starting point for Scenic Route 16, Railroad Loop and the NRAO. About 7 miles north of Marlinton on US 219 is one end of Scenic Route 15, Highland Scenic Byway.

19

Thurmond Depot

At the Bottom of the New River Gorge

General description: The drive descends into the New River Gorge to the historic railroad town of Thurmond for views of the old town and the New River, then returns via the same route to make a 20-mile trip. An optional drive for four-wheel-drive vehicles on dirt roads continues along the New River for another 13 miles for a 23-mile trip.

Location: South-central West Virginia.

Special attractions: The historic railroad depot and town of Thurmond, the New River Gorge National River, the New River itself, and the New River Gorge.

Driving route numbers: CR 25, known as McKendree Road.

Travel season: Late spring through November. Visitation is heaviest in late October when the fall colors are at their peak and on weekends in the spring and fall.

Camping: Some primitive camping is allowed on National Park Service property; check with the National Park Service for restrictions. Plum Orchard Lake Wildlife Management Area west of Glen Jean has 38 primitive campsites. Babcock State Park east of the drive has more than 50 standard campsites. At least 6 private campgrounds are clustered around the Fayetteville area. No automotive services are available along the drive. A snack and souvenir store is usually open at Thurmond during the warmer months.

Nearby attractions: Grandview State Park, Babcock State Park, Canyon Rim Visitor Center (see Scenic Route 17), and Tamarack.

The Route

Thurmond Depot, restored as a visitor center for New River Gorge National River (nps.gov/neri), is a landmark in the restored coal-shipping railroad town at the bottom of the New River Gorge. This drive, along CR 25, follows a narrow and winding two-lane paved road from Glen Jean 10 miles into the gorge to the village of Thurmond. There you can tour the old town on your own or with National Park Service rangers. A fun motorcycle ride, the steep drive is not recommended for trailers or RVs.

From Thurmond, an unimproved dirt road leads along the New River another 13 miles past numerous former mining camps to emerge on WV 41 near Grandview State Park; this makes a total trip of about 23 miles. This optional portion of the drive is recommended only for four-wheel-drive vehicles equipped for backcountry travel. If, like most visitors, you decide not to take this portion of the drive, you will retrace the drive back to Glen Jean. For that trip, the total mileage is about 20 miles.

Coal-fueled, steam-driven trains stopping for water and loads of coal made Thurmond a boomtown in the 1880s, and diesel-driven trains turned it into a

Thurmond Depot

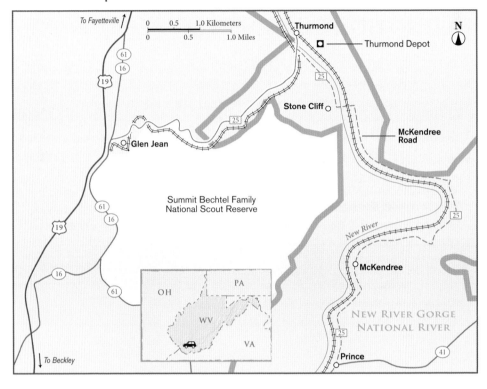

near-ghost town 50 years later. In the early 1870s, Thurmond was a sleepy settlement on a bend at the bottom of the New River Gorge. A few small coal mines enabled the residents to eke out a marginal existence.

The booming railroad industry, powered by coal-using steam engines, was bringing swift and economical transportation to many areas of the country. In 1873 the Chesapeake & Ohio Railroad main line was completed through the New River Gorge. Trains began to rumble through Thurmond, carrying coal to blast furnaces in eastern cities that produced iron around the clock to satisfy the demands of the growing nation.

Boom & Bust in Thurmond

At first Thurmond was little more than a watering stop for the trains. As more coal mines were developed in the area, the town became a shipping and loading area for the trains headed east. Water tanks and coal loading towers were built, along with a passenger depot and engine house. Soon houses dotted the steep slopes of the gorge, and to service them, hotels, banks, stores, and restaurants—even a meat

The New River near Thurmond makes for great whitewater rafting.
CLASS VI–MOUNTAIN RIVER

packing plant—sprang up. So narrow was the gorge that the town had no streets, just the railroad tracks running past the main business block.

By the early 1900s, 14 passenger and countless coal trains stopped in town daily. With coal as its mainstay, the town generated some 20 percent of all C&O revenue. Thurmond cultivated a reputation as a rough-and-tumble outlaw town, with brothels and hotels serving a heavily male population. The town had the distinction of hosting the longest-running poker game in history. The card game began in Dun Glen hotel in 1916 and ended 14 years later, but only because the hotel burned down.

The boom years ended in a whimper. In the 1930s, the Depression enveloped the country and all business slowed down. Then the C&O replaced its coal-fired locomotives with diesels. And the automobile replaced the train as the favored form of travel. Thurmond was no longer needed, and the town virtually disappeared.

Today Thurmond has only five year-round residents, and all have held town office. It is the smallest incorporated town in West Virginia. Its seclusion and the small, wooden company houses clinging to the hillside influenced movie director John Sayles to choose Thurmond as the setting for his movie *Matewan* about the 1920s miners' uprising in southern West Virginia.

Thurmond may be five breaths away from being a ghost town, but it's not lonely in the warm weather. Hikers, mountain bikers, motorbikers, cavers, anglers,

The remnants of the town of Thurmond, population 5, hug the New River.
West Virginia Department of Commerce, Stephen Shaluta

hunters, and sightseers make the downhill journey regularly. A multimillion-dollar restoration, including major repairs to the depot, has given the town much the same look it had in the 1930s and enhanced its intrigue. A museum caters to daytime guests. Visitors drive in, float in, or ride in on the Amtrak train. The Thurmond Visitor Center is open daily Memorial Day through Labor Day.

New River Joins the National Park System

In 1978 Congress added the **New River Gorge National River** (nps.gov/neri) to the National Park System, preserving Thurmond and 50 miles of the New River for all time. To begin the drive, take the Glen Jean exit from US 19 at the intersection of WV 16/61 and CR 25. Signs on CR 25 point east to Thurmond and the New River Gorge.

Glen Jean is itself the ghost of a booming mining town, though most of the original buildings (except the bank) are gone. The road passes through the hamlet in the blink of an eye and begins to parallel a creek and a railroad track, curving down in to the gorge, past woods, small groups of houses, and several one-lane bridges. The tracks and railroad siding are still used to haul coal from a small mine. After a few miles, you pass the boundary of the New River Gorge National River. Just beyond is the trailhead for the Thurmond-Minden Trail, an easy hiking and biking trail leading 3.4 miles along an old railroad bed to the town of Minden, north of Glen Jean. Highlights to this trail are a small waterfall as well as views of Thurmond and Minden.

At bottom of the gorge, signs direct you to parking. The small amount of level ground, plus heavy summer weekend visitation, has forced the National Park Service to create satellite parking areas. If visitation is light, you may be able to drive the combined road/railroad bridge across the New River to Thurmond; otherwise you can walk or take a shuttle bus to the depot.

Either way there are good views of the river, which can be a placid stream or a roaring torrent. Look for whitewater rafters approaching the bridge.

At Thurmond, your first stop should be the railroad depot just before town, where rangers lead summer tours of the Thurmond historical district. They can also help you plan your walk or hike along several trails in the vicinity.

Trains still run here, and the tracks are still the main line of the CSX, successor to the C&O Railroad. Coal and freight trains rumble through the gorge, now pulled by powerful modern diesel engines. Amtrak's passenger train, the Cardinal, passes through three times a week on its run between Washington, D.C., and Chicago. Thurmond is still a whistlestop and pickup point from rafters and climbers in the gorge. A reservation is required to board here. Rail enthusiasts plan for months to be aboard the special excursion trains that run during peak fall color. Check with Amtrak (see the appendix) for more information.

For most vehicles, Thurmond is as far as you can go on the road, and you will have to turn around and retrace the drive back to Glen Jean. You may be able to drive another 3 miles south along the New River to Stone Cliff, a popular picnicking, fishing, hiking, and swimming area when the road is open. You'll also see the cliffs that give this spot its name.

But Thurmond or Stone Cliff is the end for most vehicles. If you have a four-wheel-drive or high-centered vehicle, ask the rangers if the McKendree Road is passable. This road, a continuation of CR 25, is reached by crossing the New River via the low bridge at Stone Cliff and following the dirt road on the other side of the river. The road passes the remains of several old mining camps, including McKendree.

This section of the drive ends at Prince at the intersection with WV 41. To return to Glen Jean, turn west (right) on WV 41, and then north (right again) at WV 61 back to Glen Jean.

20

Hatfield-McCoy Country

Mountain Feuds & Coalfields

General description: A 55-mile drive along the scenic Tug Fork River to Matewan, scene of the Hatfield-McCoy feuds, and then through rugged coal country to Logan.

Special attractions: Coal House, Tug Fork River, Matewan, the Hatfield-McCoy story, coal mines, and Chief Logan State Park.

Location: Southwestern West Virginia on the Kentucky border.

Driving route numbers: US 52, 119; WV 44; CR 49, 52.

Travel season: All year.

Camping: Laurel Lake Wildlife Management Area, north of Williamson, has 25 tent sites; Chief Logan State Park has 25 sites with hookups.

Services: All at Williamson and Logan; limited at Matewan.

Nearby attractions: Laurel Creek Wildlife Management Area.

The Route

It's rough country in the southwestern corner of the state. The craggy mountains start climbing right from the river sides, often without much valley. Roads, except for a few major highways, are seldom level and twist like the tail of a pinned snake.

In 1890 the city of Williamson was farmland, one of the few flat areas among the hills. As railroads were built to haul coal from numerous productive mines, the city flourished as a rail and commercial center. Today coal is not quite the force it was 100 years ago, but it still maintains an economic importance in this city.

Decades of coal mining have left their mark on the land, but in recent years, recreation and tourism have been recognized as being almost as important as mining. As tourism has grown, interest has been regenerated in the nation's most infamous feud, spurred on by the 2012 Emmy Award–winning History Channel miniseries *Hatfields & McCoys*. The interfamily war, which was waged in the late 1800s, took place mostly in the Matewan area of southwestern West Virginia.

On this 55-mile drive, you visit the Coal House in Williamson and then follow the meandering Tug Fork of the Big Sandy River to Matewan. The drive continues through coal country, passing coal mines and coal towns to end at Logan near Chief Logan State Park.

The drive begins at the courthouse square in **Williamson,** at perhaps the most beautiful building in Mingo County: the licorice-black **Coal House.** Built entirely of coal, the building is an advertisement for coal's importance to the region's economy, history, and social structure.

Hatfield-McCoy Country

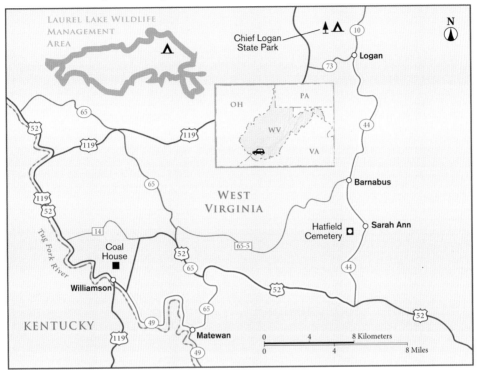

The Coal House

The shiny black rectangular building with its graceful entrance and window arches was built entirely from donations in 1933 at the height of the Depression. Sixty-five tons of local bituminous coal were carefully cut into blocks and shaped with hand tools. Even the mortar is black. The Coal House was constructed as a publicity stunt and symbol of the area's "Billion Dollar Coalfield" by the Norfolk & Western Railway. For weather protection, the outer surface is varnished every other year.

But varnish couldn't protect the Coal House from fire. Town officials and even a nationally recognized insurance company assured everyone that the building, snug up against the Mingo County Courthouse, didn't constitute a fire hazard. But burn it did on October 11, 2010. No one knows the exact origin of the fire, but it didn't appear to be arson. Luckily the coal-block exterior sustained little damage, though the walnut-paneled interior required extensive renovations. The Coal House reopened in September 2011.

Although it is known as the Coal House, the building has never been a residence. The structure is the home of the Tug Valley Chamber of Commerce, so stop by for information on other points of interest in the area. But no smoking, please.

From Williamson, go east on US 52 past the huge rail yard. You may see a line or two of coal cars today, but years ago this yard would have been filled to capacity with long trains laden with coal. About 1 mile from town, turn right on WV 49. The road and adjacent railroad follow the twisting Tug Fork of the Big Sandy River. Take time to enjoy views of the steep Kentucky banks across the water. Active coal mines are just off this road, so be alert for coal trucks.

After 15 tortuous miles, you reach **Matewan** (pronounced MATE wan), a town freighted with historical significance. The **Hatfield-McCoy feud** had been brewing since the end of the Civil War, but Matewan town became notorious in 1882 when three sons of Randolph McCoy stabbed and shot Ellison Hatfield, brother of Devil Anse Hatfield, in Pike County, Kentucky. Ellison was carried across the Tug Fork to Matewan, where he died. Devil Anse, patriarch of the Hatfield family, immediately retaliated by executing the three McCoys in Kentucky just across the river from Matewan.

Matewan's Bloody History

West Virginia bounty hunters rode into Kentucky to capture the Hatfields. The feud continued on both sides of the river for another 10 years, with retaliatory murders in both families. The bad blood between the two families had its roots in the Hatfield murder of a Union-sympathizing McCoy after the war, and it was further enflamed by a doomed romance between Randolph McCoy's daughter and Devil Anse Hatfield's son. Stories of the violence were inflated and sensationalized in national news for years, helping to spawn the image of a violent and backward Appalachia that still lingers today. The Hatfields and McCoys, though, hold a big, friendly Hatfield and McCoy Reunion Festival every June in Pikeville, Matewan, and Williamson. Forty years after the feud died down, in 1920, Matewan was again the site of violence, this time between townspeople, miners, and mine company detectives. The United Mine Workers were attempting to unionize the local coal miners. However, those who joined were summarily fired and evicted from their company-owned homes. In a dramatic showdown, Chief of Police Sid Hatfield and Mayor Cable Testermen confronted company-hired detectives who were evicting miners. Shots were fired, leaving the mayor, seven detectives, and three miners dead in the massacre.

Sid Hatfield became a hero to the miners and was acquitted of murder charges. But a year later he and a union activist were murdered by revenge-bent detectives on the steps of the courthouse in Welch. (Scenic Route 23, Coal Heritage Trail, visits Welch.) This story is told in the 1987 John Sayles movie *Matewan*. For details,

The Matewan wall adds art to the landscape.
WEST VIRGINIA DEPARTMENT OF COMMERCE, STEPHEN SHALUTA

check out the Mine Wars Museum in the old Matewan Bank. The town of Matewan was officially founded between the episodes of violence, in 1897, when the Norfolk & Western Railway opened a main line to serve the Williamson Coalfield. The town serviced the surrounding mining communities; its saloons were gathering places for miners and railroad workers to gamble and carouse.

The town today, really just 1 block long, is peaceful enough, and, in 1997, it was the first area in the coalfields to be designated a National Historic Landmark. Stop at the **Matewan Train Depot** (historicmatewan.com) for a map and guide. The depot offers lots of artifacts, pictures, and information about the Hatfield-McCoy feud, Matewan Massacre, Battle of Blair Mountain, coal mining, and railroad history. Don't miss the Old Matewan National Bank Building, with bullet holes still visible from the 1920 massacre. A recording by the bank describes the event, including recollections of elderly residents who experienced the shootings and trials firsthand. The town is also a stop along the 500-mile **Hatfield-McCoy ATV Trails System** (trailsheaven.com).

The feud still goes on but in a lighthearted way at the **Hatfield-McCoy Festival** in June. A highlight is a tug-of-war over the Tug Fork, with the Hatfields in West Virginia and the McCoys in Kentucky. The losing team gets dragged into the next state (if the river is low enough).

When you leave town, go left on WV 65 (shown as WV 9 on some maps). The road climbs out of the river valley and ends at US 52. Turn right (south). It's slow going on this winding coal-truck road, even though it is a major route.

Devil Anse's Final Resting Spot

Turn left (north) on WV 44. In Sarah Ann you pass the **Hatfield Family Cemetery** up a steep bank on the left. On the National Register of Historic Places, it is visited mostly for its life-size Italian marble statue of patriarch William Anderson "Devil Anse" Hatfield, who survived the feud and died at age 81. The statue indicates something most folks don't realize about Hatfield—he and many of his clan amassed a good fortune in the family logging business. Another surprising postscript is that Hatfield got religion and founded a Church of Christ congregation in his last decade.

Coal continues to be a major economic force in southern West Virginia, and the drive passes through several small mining communities and mines. Look for former mountaintops where the coal has been removed and attempts have been made to reseed and restructure the land. Mountaintop removal and strip mining still continue because surface mines are more economical than underground mining.

The drive ends at Logan. **Chief Logan State Park** (chiefloganstatepark.com), less than 2 miles away, is practically part of town, drawing locals and visitors alike to walk the Guyandotte Beauty Trail, swim in the pool, or enjoy a game of miniature golf. Children love observing West Virginia–native animals such as black bears, bobcats, barred owls, red-shouldered hawks, and wild boar in the wildlife park. Summer productions of the Aracoma Story as well as musicals and children's plays are staged at the park amphitheater. Aracoma, the daughter of Shawnee chief Cornstalk, married a captured British soldier in what turned out to be an ill-fated love story. The park also contains an excellent regional museum and an authentic pioneer cabin. A 75-room lodge and 25-site campground are open all year.

From Logan it is a few miles to US 119, a four-lane modern highway that will zip you back south to Williamson or north to Charleston.

Devil Anse stands tall at the Hatfield family grave in Sarah Ann.
West Virginia Department of Commerce, Stephen Shaluta

21

Athens to Lewisburg

Bluestone Gorge & Lake & Pence Springs

General description: A 52-mile drive past a 900-foot gorge and then along the meandering Greenbrier River. The drive passes steep gorges, a scenic lake, and historic buildings and towns.

Special attractions: Pipestem State Park, Bluestone National Scenic River, Bluestone State Park, Bluestone Lake and Dam, historic Hinton, John Henry monument, Pence Springs, and Lewisburg.

Location: Southern West Virginia.

Driving route numbers: US 219; WV 3, 20, 63.

Travel season: All year.

Camping: Camping is available year-round at Bluestone and Pipestem State Parks, with more than 100 sites with hookups and all conveniences. Private campgrounds near Pipestem, Hinton, Alderson, and True are open during the warmer months.

Services: All services are available in most towns along the drive.

Nearby attractions: Sandstone Falls, New River Gorge National River, and Organ Cave.

The Route

This 52-mile drive takes you from the rolling plateau near Princeton to Pipestem State Park for views of the 900-foot-deep gorge of the Bluestone National Scenic River and the many recreational facilities along Bluestone Lake. The drive passes the historic railway burg of Hinton, gateway to the New River Gorge National River. From Hinton, the drives strikes out along the Greenbrier River, past the monument to John Henry of folklore fame and a colonial-era home to an old spring at Pence Springs.

The drive continues along the Greenbrier River to end at Lewisburg, a town with roots in the Revolutionary War and buildings still peppered with Civil War bullets. The drive is over paved highways and can be made in any season.

Begin at **Athens,** just north of Princeton via WV 20. Or, from I-77 north of Princeton, take exit 14–WV 7 to WV 20. Athens is the home of **Concord College,** one of West Virginia's many small private colleges. If your timing is right, you will hear the 48 bells of its carillon ring out over the campus. The melodious sounds of these tuned bronze bells result from a gift by former Concord president Joseph Marsh. As a Dartmouth College alumnus, Dr. Marsh fondly recalled the sonorous Baker Library bells of his alma mater and made the gift of a similar carillon to Concord upon his retirement. You can hear the 15-minute mini-concerts in the late afternoons.

Athens to Lewisburg

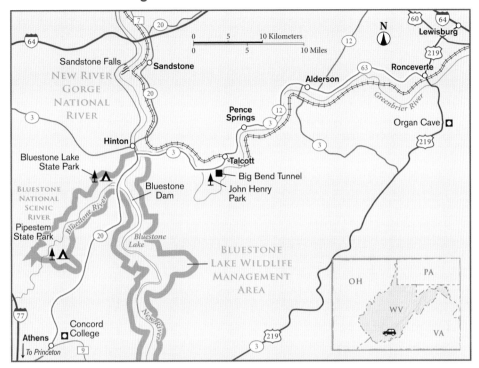

From Athens drive north on WV 20 through a quilt of woods and farmland. Note Pipestem Drive-in Theater, one of the few operating drive-ins left in the state, near the entrance to **Pipestem Resort State Park** (wvstateparks.com/park/pipestem-resort-state-park). Open weekends May through early September, the drive-in welcomes both children and pets with treats at the ticket booth.

Pipestem Resort State Park perches on the rim of the 1,000-foot gorge of the Bluestone River. Look for the park entrance about 13 miles from Athens; you can do a quick drive-through, scoping out the gorge view from several scenic overlooks and an observation tower. But if you have the time, ride the aerial tramway from the gift shop to the bottom of the gorge—it's the next best thing to flying.

If superb scenery and a tramway aren't enough, this park offers recreational activities for just about everybody: golf, fishing, dance weekends, swimming, hiking trails, outdoor concerts, canoeing, horseback riding, tennis, nature walks, ziplining tours, and, in winter, cross-country skiing. Two lodges—one on the rim, another at the bottom—a campground, cottages, and several restaurants cater to most tastes.

The 4,000-acre park lies almost entirely within the boundaries of the Bluestone National Scenic River. The bottom of the Bluestone River gorge has no roads and no trains, just hiking and horse trails that lead from the lodge. One hike even leads through the river, best done during a summer dry spell. The Bluestone gets its name from the blue-gray shale exposed in the gorge. And the pipestem bush, which gives the park its name, is a hollow woody shrub used by American Indians to make pipes.

When you leave Pipestem, turn left and continue north on WV 20. The road begins a long, gradual descent almost to river level. It crosses the Bluestone River on a high bridge at its confluence with the New River.

Bluestone's Lake & Parks

Past the bridge is the entrance to **Bluestone State Park** (wvstateparks.com/park/bluestone-state-park), which has a boat launch area, a campground, and rental cabins. Both rivers combine here to form Bluestone Lake, impounded by Bluestone Dam, which you will pass in a few minutes. The 2,000-acre elongated lake is part of yet another "Bluestone," Bluestone Lake Wildlife Management Area.

Water activities are popular here, so popular that the nearby town of Hinton celebrates a Festival of the Rivers each Labor Day. The Bluestone has excellent fishing for largemouth and smallmouth bass, crappie, and catfish. On warm weekends you'll see sailboats, powerboats, canoes, fishermen, and water-skiers, and more anglers along the shore. The road, about 75 feet above the lake, offers a good vantage point for these activities.

Ahead is the massive **Bluestone Dam.** This concrete structure rises 165 feet above the riverbed and spans 2,048 feet across the river. Construction by the US Army Corps of Engineers began in 1942, but with the intervention of World War II, it was not finished until 1952.

The dam's original purpose was flood control, but the lake soon developed into a major recreational resource. Its national significance was recognized in 1978 when the New River Gorge National River, stretching north of Hinton for 53 miles, was added to the National Park system. Scenic Routes 17 and 19 descend into the New River Gorge to explore this parkland. In 1988 the Bluestone National Scenic River was created.

About 0.5 mile past the dam, turn east (right) on WV 3, crossing the New River on the Bellepoint Bridge, near the point where the Greenbrier River flows into the New.

The town of **Hinton,** gateway to both the **Bluestone National Scenic River** (nps.gov/blue) and the New River Gorge National River (nps.gov/neri), lies to the left after you cross the bridge. Hinton's historic district includes several varieties of eclectic Victorian architecture among its homes, churches, and business buildings. The **Hinton Railroad Museum,** across the street from the New River

Swallowtail butterflies seek nectar along the New River in Hinton.

Gateway Visitor Center, explains Hinton's railroad history through vintage photographs, recordings, and train paraphernalia. Be sure to look for the 98-piece John Henry woodcarving exhibit that took a local carver three years and 20 types of wood to complete. It represents every type of 1870 railroad job that existed.

From Hinton, WV 3 follows the valley of the winding Greenbrier River, occasionally taking a shortcut over low hills. Cross the Greenbrier, turning left with WV 3 as the road merges with WV 12 north. As you come down the hill before Talcott, look for a small park on the right. A larger-than-life statue of a bare-chested black man bearing a hammer overlooks the river. This is that steel drivin' man, **John Henry,** who looks ready to pound more steel. Behind him, railroad tracks disappear into the 6,500-foot Big Bend Tunnel.

Folk songs and folklore aside, historians report that a 200-pound freed slave named John Henry did indeed help dig the tunnel for the Chesapeake & Ohio Railroad in the 1870s. But did John Henry die trying to outwork a steam drill? Probably not; more likely he was one of many killed by numerous rockfalls in the brittle shale during the building of the tunnel. During the years when the tunnel was being lined with brick, many workers claimed to have seen or heard the ghost of John Henry hammering away inside the tunnel, and to this day rumors circulate about the ghost of John Henry haunting the tunnel that supposedly took his life.

From the bottom of the hill, look back to see the portal for the original tunnel and the modern replacement with tracks. Talcott is proud of its John Henry heritage and celebrates his memory with a John Henry festival and parade each July.

Even earlier than John Henry's railroad-building days, the smoky ravines and river bottoms of southern West Virginia were a land of strong Native Americans and courageous pioneers. You get a sense of that life at the **Graham House,** on the left just north of Talcott. It's an impressive 2-story log home dating from 1770, built with security in mind—the security of the Graham family from the Shawnees, who weren't happy about Europeans in their hunting lands. In 1777, Colonel James Graham's estate was raided by Shawnees, who killed his son and carried away his young daughter. For eight years, the colonel searched for her, finally locating her in what is now Kentucky. The home, with its reinforced log walls and beams, is a National Historic Register site. Beside the Graham House stands the Saunders One-Room Schoolhouse Museum, filled with reminders of days gone by, from the hickory stick to a primer collection. The Graham House and museum are open weekend afternoons from Memorial Day through Labor Day.

Pence Springs

The hamlet of **Pence Springs** sits a few bends along the Greenbrier beyond Talcott. In 1872 Andrew Pence built a hotel beside the spring, named it and the spring after himself, and began selling the sulfur-rich mineral water. Business was slow until 1904, when the Pence Springs bottled water won a silver medal at the St. Louis World's Fair. Soon Andrew Pence was shipping several railcars of his water each week. The original hotel burned down a few years later, but Pence rebuilt in style, including such modern conveniences as telephones and showers in each room, a central vacuum system, and special accommodations for chauffeurs and maids.

Known as the Grand Hotel, it became the most expensive and most popular hotel in West Virginia, as well-heeled travelers from around the world came in on the train for relaxation, entertainment, and to imbibe the strong-tasting water. When Prohibition came along, a hidden cellar speakeasy kept liquor flowing along with the spring water. Gamblers in an adjacent underground casino celebrated their luck or drank away their troubles.

But as the Depression deepened, even bootleg liquor was not enough to keep the hotel going, and it closed in the early 1930s. The resort reincarnated as a

You can still pump the sulphuric water at Pence Spring's springhouse.

school for girls, then a short-lived dude ranch. In 1944 the state turned the property into an attractive maximum-security prison for women.

But state prison needs and standards changed. After another stint as an inn, the National Historic Register property is now occupied by the Greenbrier Academy for Girls. The spring continues to bubble forth its slightly sulfuric water under cover of the historic spring house. A popular Sunday flea market at the spring house draws bargain seekers from three states.

From Pence Springs, WV 12 continues to follow the tranquil and meandering Greenbrier River. At Alderson, known for its federal women's prison that briefly harbored Martha Stewart, the river is spanned by the stone arch of Memorial Bridge, built in 1914 and now open only to pedestrian traffic. **Alderson's Store** (aldersonsstore at Facebook) has been serving customers with grace and style since 1887. No general store with tinned meat and sprouted potatoes, Alderson's is as classy as its elegant Art Deco exterior. Inside you'll find tastefully organized collections of china, specialty books, women's clothing, and jewelry.

Bear right on WV 63 as you leave Alderson. At the intersection with US 219 in Ronceverte (French for "Greenbrier") go north (left) on US 219.

Lewisburg: Colonial & Cool

From Ronceverte, take US 219 north past the fairgrounds for the **State Fair of West Virginia** (statefairofwv.com) in Fairlea; this annual event each August attracts more than 175,000 visitors. The fairgrounds are on the outskirts of **Lewisburg,** which was first settled around 1750 and is one of the oldest towns in the state. Spirited little Lewisburg was recently voted "Coolest Small Town" in the US by a major travel magazine. It's long had a reputation as an art town. It boasts a 236-acre historic district sprinkled with cabins, 18th-century shops turned galleries, and a church with a Civil War cannonball embedded in its wall. The Old Stone Church across from Lewisburg's Carnegie Hall is the oldest Presbyterian church in continuous operation west of the Alleghenies.

Lewisburg is also known for its wacky Shanghai Parade and First Day International Festival January 1, as well as an April chocolate festival and an October food fest. Lots going on in a burgh so small you can walk anywhere, including to the town's two primo arts venues, Greenbrier Valley Theatre and Carnegie Hall.

Carnegie Hall South

Yes, **Carnegie Hall** (carnegiehallwv.org)—locals refer to the New York institution simply as "the other one." Like its Big Apple counterpart, Lewisburg's Carnegie Hall was funded by business tycoon Andrew Carnegie in the late Victorian era.

Lewisburg has its own Carnegie Hall performance and arts center.

The ornate, 4-story building is the artistic nerve center of Lewisburg, housing a dance studio, art studios, 3 art galleries, and a 500-seat auditorium for weekly drama, musical, and performance-art productions.

Three blocks away in the heart of downtown, the **Greenbrier Valley Theatre** (gvtheatre.org) draws professional actors from around the country for productions such as *Greenbrier Ghost, Suds,* and *Macbeth.*

This 52-mile drive ends in Lewisburg, off exit 169 of I-64. Scenic Route 18 continues north along the Greenbrier River.

22

Farm Heritage Road Scenic Byway

Farms & the Spas of Yesterday

General description: A 60-mile drive, part of the National Scenic Byway system, has retained the pastoral character of the last century but with a few convenience stores, gas stations, and roadside crosses testifying to our high-speed, gasoline-fueled modern era. The drive passes farms, 19th-century springs and resorts, historic towns and buildings, and mountain scenery.

Special attractions: Several former major spas and resorts, Indian Creek Covered Bridge, historical Union, Rehoboth Church, Sweet Springs Valley, and Peters Mountain.

Location: Southern West Virginia, southwest of White Sulphur Springs and I-64.

Driving route numbers: US 219; WV 3, 12, 122.

Travel season: All year. In spring redbuds (actually lavender colored) brighten up the roadsides and edges of greening forests. In fall the hillsides shine with the sun tones of oak, maple, and beech leaves.

Camping: Moncove Lake State Park, just off the drive near Gap Mills, has about 50 campsites, half with complete facilities. Bluestone State Park and Bluestone Lake Wildlife Management Area west of the drive together have more than 400 campsites; about 100 have complete facilities. Wilderness camping is permitted in the Jefferson National Forest east of Gap Mills.

Services: Gasoline and food are available in towns along the drive.

Nearby attractions: Moncove State Park, Bluestone State Park, Bluestone Lake Wildlife Management Area, Organ Cave, Hanging Rock Observatory (hawk migrations), and Jefferson National Forest.

The Route

Follow the trail of the stagecoaches carrying guests along the springs tour more than 100 years ago. Step back to a time when most folks lived on farms or in small towns. The spring spas of Monroe County once attracted thousands of visitors each year; the ailing, who came seeking relief in the mineral waters, and the rich, who came to escape the heat and socialize with the elite at luxury hotels. The **Farm Heritage Road Scenic Byway** in Monroe County visits the remnants of these former resorts, as well as historic towns, a covered bridge, and the oldest church east of the Alleghenies. The drive combines both history and scenery in a rural America that is fast disappearing.

Begin in **Peterstown** on the Virginia border, at the junction of US 219 and WV 12. Peterstown could be called West Virginia's diamond center because the only sizable diamond ever found in the state, a hefty 34-carat gem, was discovered here by William "Punch" Jones in 1928 while pitching horseshoes on the bank of

Farm Heritage Road Scenic Byway

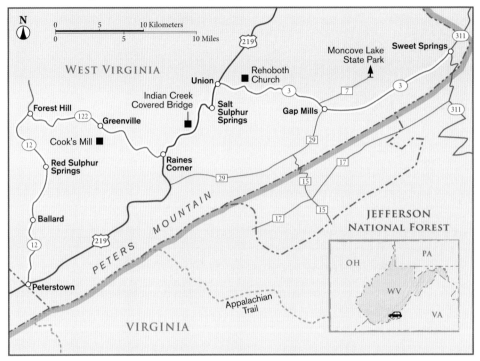

Peters Creek. The Jones diamond was large enough to get prospectors out scrambling for more. Geologists speculate that the diamond is an alluvial diamond, carried to its discovery point by streams, and that the source was to the south in Virginia. But the source—and another diamond—has never been found.

From Peterstown, go north on WV 12. The drive climbs gradually past gently rolling farmland. Look behind you to see the gap where the New River flows between Peters Mountain on the left and East River Mountain.

Red Sulphur Springs

At **Red Sulphur Springs** you come to the site of the first of several former springs resorts. The Red Sulphur Springs Hotel, built in 1832, became one of the most popular spas for people with health concerns. The resort had facilities for 550 visitors plus their horses and servants. Annual visits were touted as a means of maintaining good health. Spring water was often seen as the remedy for all manner of afflictions from skin diseases to mood disorders. Writing in the *Southern Literary Messenger* in 1835, T. W. White recommended Red Sulphur Springs water for pulmonary disease, hemorrhages, chills and fevers, asthma, consumption, night

Queen Anne's lace dapples the Monroe County meadows in July.

sweats, and a rapid pulse. It was not enough, he said, to bathe in it; readers were advised to drink a gallon of spring water every 24 hours. An excerpt from article offers a glimpse of the exalted claims made to the water's salubrious effects: "In diseases of the liver, this water is highly efficacious. In dropsy, rheumatism, gravel, gout, dyspepsia, tic doloreux, and epilepsy, it has been used with advantage. In cutaneous diseases, it seldom fails to effect a cure."

The hotel served as a military hospital during the Civil War. Like many of the springs, Red Sulphur never regained its former popularity during the hard times that followed the war. Springs also lost much of their medical appeal as people began to understand the contagious nature of many diseases, realizing that close proximity to the ill might actually make one sick. The hotel eventually closed, and all that remains is the stone spring enclosure. Looking over the small community, you would never realize that it was once a major resort.

Turn right on WV 12 at the intersection with WV 122 in Forest Hill. Just before Greenville is the site of Cook's Fort, which covered more than an acre and reputedly protected more than 300 settlers from an Indian attack in 1778. Like the Red Sulphur Springs hotel, nothing remains of the fort today. Nearby, the 1867 **Cook's Mill** (cooksoldmill.com) stands on its old mill pond in perfectly restored working order. Construction elements include hand-hewn, mortise-and-tenon posts and beams.

The original mill was built in this same spot in 1796. The present owner plans to develop the mills and surrounding buildings as a center for artisans using traditional techniques. The adjacent forge building contains blacksmithing equipment, and occasional demonstrations take place in the summer. The owners have created a picturesque setting where vistors can picnic.

Where there are springs and limestone, you usually find caves, and Monroe County has an extensive network of these underground wonders. Some, such as the Greenville Cave (closed to the public), were mined for saltpeter in the early 1800s and during the Civil War. Chemically, saltpeter is potassium nitrate, vital in frontier days for the manufacture of gunpowder. It crystalized on cave walls and showed up in the accumulations of bat guano on the cave floor. The "peter dirt" was stored in wooden hoppers and hauled out on mule-drawn carts. The wooden hoppers and cart tracks in the cave floor can still be seen in the Greenville and Organ caves.

WV 122 ends at the intersection with US 219. Turn north (left). This US highway runs northeast–southwest for some 150 miles past much of the state's prettiest mountain scenery along the Allegheny Front, from Peterstown, West Virginia, to Maryland. It follows the Seneca Trail or Warrior's Trail, an ancient American Indian pathway, through much of the southeast to New York State.

Indian Creek Covered Bridge

The **Indian Creek Covered Bridge** sits beside US 219 a few miles north. The bridge could be considered a monument to youthful labor and ingenuity. It was constructed around 1900 by the two Weikle brothers when they were still teenagers. The 50-foot restored bridge is no longer used by highway traffic but is open for pedestrians.

Perhaps the Weikles built the bridge to ease the way for stagecoaches to reach **Salt Sulphur Springs,** less than a mile downstream of the bridge. With many of the original buildings still standing, the Salt, as it was called, is the best preserved springs resort on the drive. The soothing waters of Salt Sulphur Springs, near Union, were discovered in 1805. A stone bathhouse and main hotel were built about 1820.

Isaac Caruthers and William Erskine turned the property into a popular resort at a time when mineral waters were considered a cure for headaches, neuralgia, and other health problems. Salt Sulphur waters were described by historian Oren F. Morton as "chalybeate and sweetly sulphurous and containing iodine." Modern analysis shows the principal minerals to be sulfate, calcium, bicarbonate, and sodium. A notable visitor in 1844 was US senator John C. Calhoun, a South Carolinian who advocated the right of states to nullify federal legislation.

Salt Sulphur Springs resort is the state's largest pre-Civil War stone complex.

The resort closed during the Civil War, when the property was used by both armies for rest stops. In 1882, Colonel J. W. M. Appleton revived Salt Sulphur, but the mineral-springs vacation trade declined at the turn of the century and never really revived. The hotel is now a private residence with an adjacent guesthouse.

The resort complex, on a curve of the highway 2 miles south of Union, is one of the largest groupings of antebellum native stone buildings in West Virginia. The resort is on the National Historic Register.

Just up the hill, the town of **Union** (union.net) has the time-pocket look of a well-preserved rural community. Some 46 antebellum buildings are preserved in its historical district, including an 1810 log house and one of the state's first African-American Methodist churches. Stop at the Monroe County Historical Society Museum for its historical exhibits and the brochure for a self-guiding walking tour. The tour includes the Green Hill Cemetery, where soldiers from both the Revolutionary and Civil Wars are interred. Almost the entire town is on the National Register of Historic Places.

Union: For the Confederacy or Union?

Visitors driving north through Union see the big Confederate monument in the field just off Main Street and scratch their heads. "What's this doing here?"

Actually the village was Union long before the Civil War began. The Monroe County town was settled in 1774, chartered in 1799, and named Union because its massive oak tree was a rendezvous site for troops gathering during the French and Indian War. Although this county was claimed by the West Virginia faction when they split from Virginia to side with the Union in 1861, Union itself probably had more Confederate than Union sympathizers. The village produced General John Echols, commander of Confederate forces in the Kanawha Valley, and Captain Hugh Tiffany, the first Confederate officer killed in the war.

Though both armies passed through town repeatedly, they were kind to Union. It wasn't until 1894 that the idea for a Civil War monument came up, at a Confederate reunion in Union. Why the monument was banished to the end of Main Street is not really known. Some say the town was expected to grow out to meet it; others postulate a pro-Northern majority of town leaders made the Southerners place their statue out of town.

"It wasn't their intention to have it out there by itself," said *Monroe Watchman* editor Craig Mohler, who claims both Union and Confederate forbears. "That I'm sure of."

Rehoboth Church, Oldest West of the Alleghenies

When you leave Union, turn east (right) on WV 3, leaving US 219. After 2 miles, turn left at the sign for **Rehoboth Church.** Since 1786, the little church has been sitting in the bottom of a dimple in Monroe County's rolling hills, hidden to road travelers. Built when Shawnee Indians raided the region, the log church is sited so that no one can slip within rifle-shot range unseen. Some say it was constructed to double as a fort, or at least a refuge.

Rehoboth is the oldest Protestant church building west of the Allegheny Mountains. The church was dedicated by the famed Methodist circuit rider Bishop Francis Asbury. An iron plaque declares it a place for worship "as long as the grass grows and water flows."

What appears to be the roof now is a modern external metal shelter that protects the original wooden roof below. Although regular services are no longer held in the small, dim building, Rehoboth does open up its plank doors for special occasions such as historical services. The original pulpit remains, but the old book board is gone, split long ago by the fist of a rousing preacher. At barely 600 square feet, the structure's interior is too small to house two medium-size cars. Still, it was larger than any of the homes where local Methodists had previously been meeting.

The tiny church is now a designated United Methodist shrine and on the National Register of Historic Places. Ironically, the church plot was donated by a

Roman Catholic settler, Edward Keenan, who was sympathetic to the Methodists. Keenan's tombstone is located beside those of former Revolutionary War soldiers in the Rehoboth Church cemetery.

A small museum and conference center sits adjacent to the original church. The museum displays significant historical artifacts from the region, including Rehoboth's battered, poplar communion table. The museum is open Friday, Saturday, and Sunday afternoons during the late spring and summer.

The hilly farmland between Union and Gap Mills has few surface streams; most of the drainage is underground. Rain water percolates into the limestone rock, picking up various minerals and emerges at lower elevations as one of the numerous springs.

A short distance down US 219, a roadside sign describes the "BIG LIME OF THE DRILLER." This refers to the thick limestones of the Mississippian age Greenbrier formation. Drillers like the Greenbrier stone because oil and gas are often found far underground in this formation, covered by younger rocks. Cave explorers like the Greenbrier because numerous caves are found in this formation when it is close to the surface. Here and elsewhere in eastern West Virginia, the Greenbrier formation forms concrete-gray outcroppings.

WV 3 leads you through two gaps in the low hills. Between the two is a road on the left leading to **Moncove Lake State Park** (wvstateparks.com/park/moncove-lake-state-park).

The park offers fishing, camping, and picnicking at a secluded lake. The 144-acre lake contains largemouth bass, bluegill, catfish and trout, and rowboats and paddleboats can be rented.

Past the second gap is the town of **Gap Mills.** Once known for the several water-powered mills that operated here, the town is now populated by Mennonites, who run a cheese and spice shop, a bakery, a cabinet shop, and Yoder's Country Kettle jam company. At this point, you have the opportunity to take a short side trip to the top of **Peters Mountain.** If it is early fall—hawk migration season—I highly recommend it. At Gap Mills, veer right (south) on CR 15, the Mountain's Shadow Trail Scenic Byway, along Peters Mountain. In about 2 miles, turn left again, still on CR 15, to shoot up the mountain to a 1.5-mile footpath at the top leading to **Hanging Rock Observatory** (hangingrocktower.org). The shelter braced on a rock outcropping atop the 3,800-foot ridge is the perfect vantage for watching raptors' fall migration or just enjoying the vista. Visitors from 24 states have recorded their observations of eagles, hawks, osprey, and falcons at the observatory's website. The broad-winged hawk is the most commonly sighted bird.

Old Sweet Springs' pool was used by George Washington, Patrick Henry, and Robert E. Lee.

Returning to the valley, retrace your path and follow WV 3 northeast (right) into the broad, open farmlands of Sweet Springs Valley.

The drive gradually climbs until it reaches the Great Eastern Divide. Ahead, the streams flow eventually into the James River and Chesapeake Bay. Behind you, all water flows into the New River, and eventually the Ohio and Mississippi Rivers.

Old Sweet Springs, at the end of our drive, pops out of the rural landscape like a West Virginia Versailles. Reputedly designed by Thomas Jefferson, the massive Georgian colonial hotel was constructed in 1833. George Washington did sleep in the original old hotel, built in 1792, as did James Madison and Patrick Henry. Virginia governor John Floyd is still sleeping here, in the Sweet Spring Cemetery. Although several owners have tried to renovate the hotel, classical bathhouse, and several 2-story guest houses, the expense proved overwhelming. Now Ashby Berkley, who renovated Pence Springs in the 1980s, has purchased "Old Sweet" and is leading the charge to put her back on her feet. The nonprofit he formed to restore the property hosts fundraisers, including murder mysteries, music festivals, ox roasts, and a haunted house.

The drive ends here, about 1 mile from the Virginia line. You can retrace the drive, or continue straight ahead on VA 311. Just past the state boundary is privately owned **Sweet Chalybeate Springs,** one of the secondary springs resorts in the area. Now the pool, gazebo, and bathhouse are hidden behind a high wire fence, but you can glimpse the stream of Chalybeate water, which means "tasting like iron." From there, you can continue on curvy VA 311, which intersects with I-64/US 60 a few miles south of White Sulphur Springs.

23

Coal Heritage Trail

Bluefield to Beckley

General description: A 97-mile, winding drive from Bluefield to Beckley through the heart of coal country past mining camps and mine owners' mansions, coal mines, tipples, and company stores.

Special attractions: Pinnacle Rock State Park, Bramwell, coal mining camps and equipment, and WWI Memorial for African Americans.

Location: Southern West Virginia.

Driving route numbers: US 19, 52; WV 16.

Travel season: All year.

Camping: Twin Falls State Park has 50 campsites, most with hookups, and is open during the warmer months. Camp Creek State Park has 36 tent/trailer sites. Beckley has several private campgrounds.

Services: All services are plentiful in Bluefield and Beckley. Gas and food are available in most towns along the drive.

Nearby attractions: New River Gorge, Tamarack, Grandview State Park outdoor dramas, Twin Falls State Park, Beckley Exhibition Coal Mine, and Pocahontas (Virginia) Exhibition Mine.

The Route

Millions of years ago huge swamps covered much of West Virginia. Organic material was compacted under thousands of feet of sedimentary deposits. Eventually it was converted into a soft, black, mostly carbon rock—coal, the rock that powered US industry.

In the 1870s the Norfolk & Western (N&W) and the Chesapeake & Ohio (C&O) railroads reached the huge coalfields of southern West Virginia. Almost overnight, communities became boom towns, and the fortunate mine owners found themselves millionaires.

This 97-mile drive passes through the heart of coal country in southern West Virginia. You'll see the ornate mansions of the mine owners and row after row of miners' small houses. You'll also see the infrastructure that served mining—tipples, company stores, and huge railroad yards in the narrow stream valleys. The drive is entirely on two-lane, paved roads that are often used by coal trucks.

Bluefield, West Virginia, is the larger of two towns with the same name straddling the Virginia–West Virginia border near the center of the famed Pocahontas Coalfield. This coal—low in sulfur, high in carbon—became the standard by which all other bituminous coal was measured. It helped drive the Industrial Revolution worldwide and powered US Navy ships in both World War I and the Spanish-American War. Rail fans will want to visit Bluefield's extensive railroad yards, which featured "natural gravity" loading. Bluefield flourished as the de facto

Coal Heritage Trail

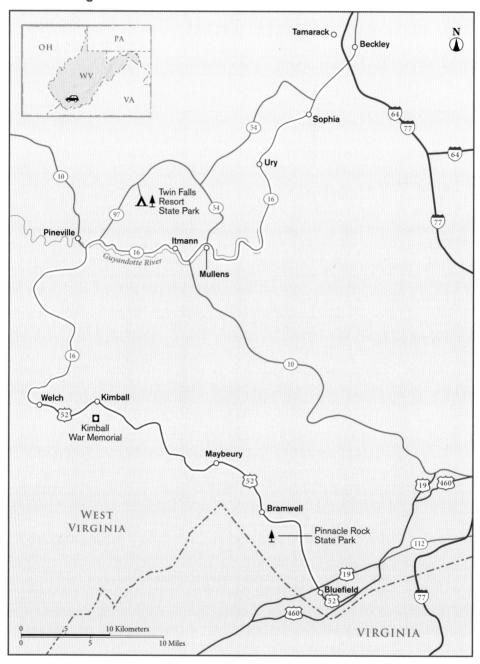

capital of the southern West Virginia and Virginia coalfields from 1900 to the 1920s.

Bluefield's historic city hall building, now known as the **Bluefield Area Arts Center** (bluefieldartcenter.com), is an elegant venue featuring the Summit Players' live theater. Nearby is the Eastern Regional Coal Archives, with an extensive collection of coal-mining material, from miners' tools to old photographs to company records and correspondence. The **Ramsey School** building was listed in Ripley's Believe It or Not for its seven entrances on seven different levels. Its most notable tenant, Gary Bowling's House of Art, features zany, interesting art from all over Appalachia. One of the city's claims to fame is tied to its geography rather than its coal geology. The highest city east of Denver, at 2,612 feet, Bluefield's chamber of commerce serves free lemonade to all on the rare days when noontime temperatures reach 90 degrees. But Bluefield's glittering winter landscape also attracts visitors. The holiday season brings 600,000 lights, strung up throughout Tony Lotitio City Park, where the Holiday of Lights has become an annual event.

East River Mountain dominates the city's skyline along the boundary between Virginia and West Virginia. If you have the time, drive to the **East River Mountain Scenic Overlook** (take WV 598 off US 460) for a bird's-eye view of the city and surrounding mountains from 3,500 feet. This is also the midpoint of a loop drive between Bluefield and Wytheville, Virginia, described in Globe Pequot Press's FalconGuide *Scenic Routes & Byways Virginia*.

This drive heads west on US 52. After a few strip malls, you soon come to **Pinnacle Rock State Park** (pinnaclerockstatepark.com). This pointy crag of sandstone effectively marks the end of the sandstone/limestone topography and the beginning of shale coal country. To the east you'll see more farms, and to the west mines and mined-over hills predominate. A compact wayside park with a 2-mile trail down to 15-acre Jimmy Lewis Lake, Pinnacle is a product of the Works Progress Administration (WPA). Its stone walkways, fireplaces, and green shelters were built in 1938. About 5 miles from Bluefield is the turnoff for Bramwell (rhymes with "camel"), once considered the richest town in the US. **Bramwell** was home to 15 millionaires within a 2-block radius, made wealthy by the underground toils of others. In the early 1900s they built opulent Victorian-style mansions with copper roofs, inlaid Italian marble stonework, electric servant call bells, and even an indoor swimming pool.

Bramwell, Richest Town in the Country

The wealthy residents of **Bramwell** (bramwellwv.com) enjoyed an active social life, but if life in town grew boring, 14 trains stopped daily at the town station, including 3 to New York. The tiny Bank of Bramwell had the highest deposits per

Bramwell's restored depot functions as an interpretive center for the town.

capita of any bank in the country; with all that money entrusted to it, it financed projects far from its doors, including the prestigious Burning Tree Country Club outside Washington, D.C.

But all good rides come to an end. When the stock market crashed in 1929, so did many fortunes. The buildings remain, nearly all of them well preserved today. In 1983 the entire town was placed on the National Register of Historic Places. The restored train station is now a visitor center where you can pick up a tour guide and plan your visit. Three weeks before Christmas and on Mother's Day weekend, various Bramwell organizations conduct guided tours of the town's mansions; check out the town's website for more information.

As you leave Bramwell and head west on US 52, look into the forest on your left for the remnants of a line of old beehive coke ovens. These coal-processing kilns created a valuable coal by-product while polluting the air to near toxic levels.

Past Bramwell on US 52 the valleys narrow and the hills become closer and steeper. At road cuts, look for black seams of coal in the flat-lying rocks. The road passes through small mining camps such as Elkhorn, with its attractive green and white company housing and gold-domed Russian Orthodox church.

More than 100,000 miners toiled in West Virginia's coalfields during the boom years. Miners came from all over, including African Americans fleeing the Deep South and Eastern European immigrants seeking a better life in the New World. A century ago coal mining was laborious, dangerous hand work. Highly mechanized mining today requires fewer workers for more output. Some 500 small company camps have been recognized along the Coal Heritage Trail, many of them just remnants and a few only marks on the map. Isolated as they were, miners were part of tight communities, with scant attention paid to racial or ethnic differences.

World War I Memorial for African-American Veterans

Perched on a hill above US 52, the **Kimball War Memorial** (forgottenlegacywwi .org) tells the little-known story of African-American military service during the War to End All Wars, World War I.

The 2-story building fronted by four huge terra-cotta columns was built in 1928, when a group of black veterans successfully petitioned the McDowell County Commission for construction funds after a memorial to white veterans was erected at the county courthouse in Welch.

About 1,500 African-American men from McDowell County were among the 400,000 black servicemen who enlisted to fight for the Allied cause after the US entered the war in 1917. When allowed to fight, these soldiers did so with honor, demonstrating their valor in combat beside with French forces. As a result 171 black soldiers were awarded the Legion of Honor medal, France's highest decoration. Thirteen hundred were commissioned as US military officers for their services during World War I.

After falling into neglect and then being gutted by a suspicious fire, the nation's only memorial to African-American World War I veterans has been revived, thanks to a $1.6 million renovation and an interactive museum exhibit prepared by West Virginia University students and faculty. The building is also the site of the first black American Legion post and has hosted Cab Calloway's band and other notables.

Most tourists visiting Welch, 4 miles west, make a beeline for **McDowell County Courthouse,** with its 3-story clock tower. It was on the front steps of this building, on August 1, 1921, that detectives hired by coal-company officials gunned down Matewan police chief Sid Hatfield and union activist Ed Chambers in retaliation for the deaths of two of their colleagues at the Matewan Massacre a year earlier. (See Scenic Route 20, Hatfield-McCoy Country, for more about this incident.) The courthouse killings touched off a series of events that led to the Battle of Blair Mountain in neighboring Logan County, in which 10,000 miners took up arms against coal-company officials. It was the largest insurrection in the US since the Civil War, and it ended only when federal troops were called in after as many as 130 men, women, and children were killed.

Turn north (right) on WV 16 in Welch. This road has less traffic and fewer towns than the first part of the drive. You'll experience a little straighter path, but much more up and down. Pass through several small mining communities and along Indian Creek. At the county seat of Pineville, population 700, you have the opportunity to take a 0.5-mile side trip into town for a glimpse of **Castle Rock.** Located beside the town library at 124 Castlerock Ave., the rock rises about 200 feet above Rock Castle Creek. A railed staircase in the rock leads to a stone terrace midway up.

As you follow the Guyandotte River 7 miles to Itmann, the results of intensive coal mining are evident. In some places, trees are just becoming reestablished. The palatial company store in **Itmann** (named for Bramwell banker I. T. Mann) verges on lovely, even in its neglected modern state. The structure was built between 1923 and 1925 by more than 100 Italian stonemasons, who quarried the stone from a site across the river and hauled it to the store block by block. The store was operated by the Pocahontas Fuel Co. (now CONSOL), which also operated the state's most productive mine at Itmann.

The mine and company store closed in the 1980s, and the landmark building has served as a homeless shelter and a veteran's hall. It has been purchased by a private owner and stands empty at present.

Many of the small, prefab homes that went up in 1918 to serve the miners are still occupied.

Mullens, the next town on the route, was nearly destroyed by a flash flood in 2001. While the town has attempted to redevelop with the aid of state and federal recovery money, many local businesses and residents have simply fled this former mining and railroad town. Although Mullens is the mailing address for **Twin Falls Resort State Park** (wvstateparks.com/park/twin-falls-resort-state-park), it is actually a counterclockwise drive about 12 miles north of town over WV 54 and WV 97. The park features a resort lodge with an indoor pool and 18-hole champion golf course. One of the 9 hiking trails leads past the namesake waterfalls, as well as the remnants of an early mill. A campground is open from Easter through October.

WV 16 continues deep into mining country. Note the mined-over area sprouting new growth as the road climbs the long slope after crossing the railroad tracks in Ury. Sophia is the childhood home of the late senator Robert Byrd, longest-serving member of the US Senate. The town hosts a Community Gospel Nights festival each June.

WV 16 continues to exit 42 of I-64/77 and the end of the drive at Beckley. You may want to cap off your drive with a tour of the Beckley Exhibition Mine or a visit to Tamarack, the state's showcase for the arts and crafts. Beckley is also the gateway for excursions into the New River Gorge. For a fast trip back to Bluefield, take I-77 south.

The falls of Twin Falls Resort State Park can be reached in a short hike.

24

The Best of the Midland Trail

Old US 60

General description: An 81-mile drive on US 60 over the middle two-thirds of the Midland Trail Scenic Highway from Sam Black Church to Malden, past historical sites, views of the New River Gorge, falls, and the Kanawha River.

Special attractions: Meadow River Wildlife Management Area, Babcock and Hawks Nest State Parks, New River Gorge National River, Kanawha and Cathedral Falls, and African Zion Baptist Church.

Location: South-central West Virginia.

Driving route numbers: US 60, the Midland Trail.

Travel season: All year.

Camping: Babcock State Park has 52 sites, most with hookups. Private campgrounds are located near White Sulphur Springs, Hico, Glen Jean, and Fayetteville.

Services: All services are available along the drive.

Nearby attractions: Lewisburg, Lost World Caverns, New River Gorge National River, Gauley River National Recreation Area, Carnifex Ferry Battlefield State Park, New River rafting outfitters, New River Bridge Walk, and Charleston.

The Route

The **Midland Trail Scenic Highway** follows US 60 from the Virginia border to the Kentucky border near Kenova, West Virginia Once part of the main transcontinental highway system, US 60 became a secondary route for local traffic after completion of I-64 in 1988.

From its beginnings as a buffalo trail and Indian footpath through European Americans' westward migration, the Midland Trail has been an important east–west artery. The Midland Trail became part of the first transcontinental motor route. US 60 today has been restored to its rightful place in history and designated the Midland Trail Scenic Highway.

Blue byway mile markers indicate the way along the trail from the Ohio-Kentucky border at Kenova to the Virginia border near White Sulphur Springs. Our tour describes the trail's 81 miles from Sam Black Church at I-64's exit 156 to Malden, just off exit 96 of I-64/77 near Charleston.

Start at **Sam Black Church.** The actual church is south of the interstate interchange. Reverend Sam Black (1813–1899) was a Methodist circuit rider for nearly 50 years. The church, built in 1901, was dedicated to Black, and the unincorporated community bears his name. Although Sam Black's long, hard struggle to spread the word of God to the mountains truly deserves memorialization, the community is just as well known as the site of the **Greenbrier Ghost.** A state historic marker telling the story appears 0.25-mile east of the church. The way

The Best of the Midland Trail

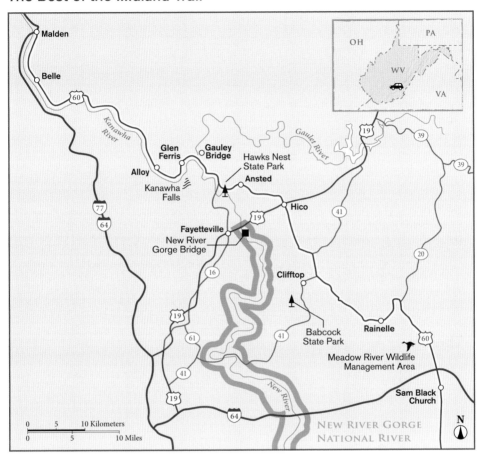

Lewisburg ghost-tour leaders tell it, West Virginia's most famous ghost, a woman named Zona Shue, returned from the grave to reveal to her mother that she had been murdered by her husband. Her mother told the tale to everyone who would listen, prompting authorities to exhume her daughter's body. Sure enough, Zona had a compound fracture in her neck, and Shue's husband eventually was convicted of her murder.

From the church go north on US 60. In 5 miles, look for the sign on Tommy Hall Road pointing left to **Meadow River Wildlife Management Area.** During the spring and fall migrations, this large wetland is an important stop for waterfowl, including mallards, teals, and wood ducks. In spring listen for the call of several species of frogs, including spring peepers, bull frogs, pickerel frogs, and green frogs.

The long uphill stretch past Rainelle winds up the slopes of 3,211-foot Sewell Mountain with 156 curves in 11 miles; this section of the Midland Trail is a fun park for motorcyclists. Views are spectacular, and, luckily for drivers, overlooks are located at strategic points. On the eastern slope near Maywood, you'll see the fenced Lee's Tree, where Confederate General Robert E. Lee camped during the Battle of Big Sewell and where he first met his beloved warhorse, Traveller.

Babcock State Park

At Clifftop, just past mile 117, WV 41 goes left 4 miles to **Babcock State Park** (wvstateparks.com/park/babcock-state-park) at the edge of the New River Gorge. Its 20 miles of hiking trails lead to numerous overlooks into the New River Gorge National River (nps.gov/neri). (Scenic Routes 17 and 19 explore the New River Gorge National River from points several miles south.) At frequently photographed Glade Creek Grist Mill, you can watch the waterwheel turn and buy freshly ground cornmeal.

Nearby is Camp Washington-Carver, better known to fans of old-time music as Clifftop. Originally built as the nation's first African-American 4-H camp by the Civilian Conservation Corps, the state-run site features several music festivals including an annual **Appalachian String Band Festival** (wvculture.org/stringband) that draws international participants.

Back on the trail, you pass **Spy Rock** at an elevation of 2,500 feet, used as an observation point by early Indians and during the Civil War by both Union and Confederate troops. Some say the town of Lookout (the start of Scenic Route 17) got its name from the sandstone outcropping. At Hico, you pass the intersection with US 19; a few miles south on US 19 Scenic Route 17 ends at the Canyon Rim Visitor Center and the New River Gorge Bridge.

The village of **Ansted** is steeped in history: A coal baron's mansion, the Page Vawter House; Civil War trail markers; and Contentment House Museum, an 1830 home sheltering the Fayette County Historical Society are all right off the highway. West of Ansted, be sure to stop at **Hawks Nest State Park** (wvstateparks.com/park/hawks-nest-state-park) for dramatic views on the rim of the New River Gorge. A tramway descends into the gorge where, in summer, you can take a jet-boat ride upstream almost to the base of the New River Gorge Bridge, 976 feet above the water. Those feeling more energetic can follow several trails along the rim or to the bottom of the gorge. An exceptional rail trail leads from the gorge floor up to Ansted, past an old mine and several small waterfalls. The lodge and restaurant allow you to watch the sunset over the New River from your table or room.

If you look west, you'll see a large dam. In an engineering feat, more than 3,000 men drilled through Gauley Mountain in the 1930s. They diverted part of

The lodge at Hawks Nest State Park is renowned for its views of the New River.

the New River into a conduit to turbines that generate electricity for the Elkem Metals facility downriver at Alloy. Drilling the tunnel resulted in one of the worst industrial disasters in US history. The project took the lives of at least 476 workers, many of them migrant African Americans, who died from the lung disease silicosis after inhaling silica dust in the tunnel.

If you look below the dam, you'll see what is known as "the Dries," a 5.5-mile rocky river bottom dotted with small pools of water—what is left after perhaps nine-tenths of the river is diverted through the tunnel under Gauley Mountain. The diverted water reemerges at Hawks Nest Hydro plant near Gauley Bridge, on your left as you descend the mountain to the river. You can park in a small lot here and walk down to a set of stairs that leads along the side of the plant and over the reemerging river. This scenic area is a popular fishing spot.

On the opposite side of the road at mile 97, you'll see the cascading Cathedral Falls. A small parking area and path allow you a closer look at the moss-covered rocks and pool at the bottom. At Gauley Bridge, the New and the Gauley Rivers unite to form the wide Kanawha River, which you follow for the rest of the drive.

The **Glen Ferris Inn,** built in 1810 as a home, was the first permanent building constructed in Glen Ferris. In 1839, it became the Stockton Inn and received such famous guests as Andrew Jackson, John Tyler, Henry Clay, and John James Audubon. During the Civil War, it hosted officers from both sides. The Federal-style inn offers meals and lodging overlooking the wide Kanawha Falls; a small park below the falls is a favorite fishing and picnic area.

The drive continues downstream along the broad flood plain, becoming increasingly more industrial. The road is level, with no major curves. Alloy is

dominated by a modern ferro-alloy plant. Many of the small towns are former coal camps, some still serving working mines and processing plants. At one point a conveyor crosses over the highway and extends up into the bluffs.

In 1938 the US Army Corps of Engineers built a series of locks and dams along the Kanawha to smooth out the 9-foot drop between Kanawha Falls and Charleston. The easiest one to view is at London, although security requirements confine your viewing to the opposite side of a chain-link fence.

West of Belle, US 60 becomes a four-lane highway. You can continue along the Midland Trail on the old road, which parallels the highway, to Malden, mile 4.

Booker T. Washington & Early Industry

During the 19th century, **Malden** was the center of the booming salt industry where the J.Q. Dickinson Salt Works produces table salt today and was known as Kanawha Salines. Slaves carried out much of the salt manufacturing before the Civil War; after the war many worked as free men. They worshipped in the African Zion Baptist Church, founded in 1863. The present frame church was built in 1872 and is on the National Register of Historic Places.

The most famous member of this congregation is African-American educator **Booker T. Washington.** Born as a slave in Virginia, 9-year-old Washington and his family walked 225 miles to Malden when they were freed after the Civil War. He labored in the salt works with his stepfather, eventually becoming a garden helper for the wealthy Ruffner family, who encouraged his education. After attending Hampton Institute in Virginia, Washington returned to Malden, where he married and served as schoolmaster. He left several years later to serve as headmaster of the Tuskegee Institute in Alabama, becoming "the most important leader of any race to come out of the South after the Civil War," people said at his death in 1915. Although his original home is no longer standing, West Virginia State University maintains a replica of the small cabin where he lived and the schoolhouse he attended, both behind the church where he learned to read. A small public park and monument also honor him here. Washington's groundbreaking book, *Up from Slavery,* describes his life in Malden.

The drive ends here at Malden near exit 96 of I-64/77. You can also continue on US 60 and the Midland Scenic Trail into Charleston to the state capitol.

Civilian Conservation Corps architecture at Hawks Nest State Park includes a bathroom tower.

25

Greenbrier Rocks & Rivers

Clear-Flowing Rivers & Dramatic Rock Folds

General description: A 62-mile drive through some uncharacteristically level land in southeastern West Virginia, through bluegrass pastureland, past a large cave, and beside both the Greenbrier River and The Greenbrier resort, as well as Monongahela National Forest. The route starts in Union, passing a large Confederate monument and the antebellum Caperton mansion at the edge of town, traveling through a karst terrain underlain with caverns to a labyrinth depicting the course of the Greenbrier River, then follows a section of the old Midland Trail through White Sulphur Springs. You'll see a modern springs resort as well as a national fish hatchery, then travel north along national forest to an interesting geological feature on Knapp's Creek.

Special attractions: Historic buildings, Organ Cave, Greenbrier RiverWise, Greenbrier River Trail, The Greenbrier resort, White Sulphur Springs National Fish Hatchery, Allegheny Trail, Huntersville Anticline.

Location: Southeastern West Virginia, east of Lewisburg, West Virginia, off I-64.

Driving route numbers: US 60, 219; WV 63, 92.

Travel season: All year. WV 92, one of the flattest secondary roads in the Mountain State, is used by chartered buses headed north to the ski resorts.

Camping: Organ Cave has 34 sites with full facilities. Greenbrier State Forest has 16 campsites, while Blue Bend and Blue Meadow in Monongahela National Forest offer 21 and 17 sites, respectively, with partial facilities. Seneca State Forest has 10 campsites, while Watoga State Park has 100.

Services: Gasoline and food are available in Union, Pickaway, and White Sulphur Springs.

Nearby attractions: Moncove State Park, Lewisburg historic district, Greenbrier State Forest, Blue Bend swimming hole, Seneca State Forest, and Monongahela National Forest.

The Route

Union (also the midpoint of Scenic Route 22) is a wonderful find of a town, chock-full of historical buildings, completely walkable, and not a stoplight to be seen in the whole county. Walking-tour brochures can be picked up at the Monroe Historical Society museum on Main Street. When you're ready to start the drive, head northwest on US 219. As you round the bend by the Confederate monument, look right toward the magnificent wedding-cake house on the hillside. Hugh Caperton, who built Elmwood in 1835, was a prominent figure in regional politics, and his descendants continued that tradition—20th century West Virginia governor Gaston Caperton was in his line. Hugh Caperton's grandson, who lived in Elmwood during the Civil War, served as a Confederate

172

Greenbrier Rocks & Rivers

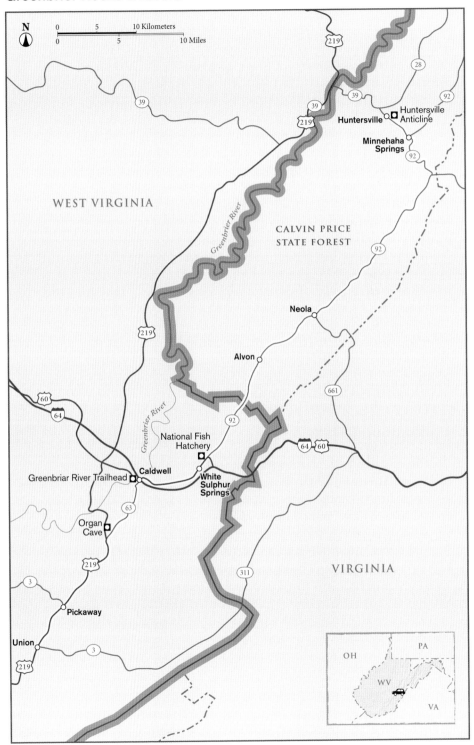

senator for Virginia. While Caperton's livestock was plundered when, in 1864, Union General Crook's 10,000 men camped in surrounding fields, Elmwood was spared burning, as well all of Union. More than 30 unscathed antebellum structures stand in the town. The 1810 Wiseman House on Main St., furnished with local antiques, is part of the Monroe County Historical Society. A carriage museum next door contains a collection of 19th century, horse-drawn vehicles.

As you continue northwest on US 219, you will see the Knobs, the low mountains where many town residents hid as General Crook approached. In the tree line straight ahead, you may spot Walnut Grove, a 1771 Greek Revival home that served as a hospital when Crook's forces occupied the area. When many single shoes were found under the house later, people decided they were likely tossed there after amputations.

You continue the drive through rolling hills. Mountains remain within view, but your path is relatively smooth; this area was once known as "Pickaway Levels." As you enter the hamlet of Pickaway, look to the left for a historic sign by a small white building. It marks the location of West Virginia's first "Corn Club." This forerunner of the 4-H club provided the local schoolchildren with tested corn seed, which they raised for exhibition at the county "corn show." Many of the names on Pickaway mailboxes were the same then as they are now, descendants of families who settled the area more than 200 years ago. Beckett, one of those names, is also the name of a small wayside park. This relic of a bygone era features picnic tables, swings, an outhouse, and a ball field.

Underground Wonder

Back on US 219, after 2 miles start looking for the right-hand turn to Organ Cave on WV 63. The Organ Cave community schoolhouse building, also on the right, is your landmark. The driveway for the commercial cave and its adjacent campground is less than 0.25 mile on your right.

On a cool morning, **Organ Cave** (organcave.com) exudes a warm mist from its rocky mouth. About 100 steps down its gullet you're enveloped in eternal cave night. If you're on the regular historical tour, there will be a lighted pathway. You'll see the hoppers used by Confederate soldiers when they mined saltpeter here during the Civil War. You'll also see statues of gray-coated soldiers pushing those hoppers, but don't look too closely—they are reincarnated store mannequins with cave mold in their hair. When Thomas Jefferson visited this cave in the late 1700s, he discovered several fossils. Since then the cave has proven a trove of Pleistocene and Pliocene mammal fossils, including a saber-toothed cat and American mastodon.

If you're game to try one of Organ Cave's wild tours, switch on your headlamp and say good-bye to the world of colors. Down here, where nothing changes much for centuries, you'll come to appreciate a much narrower band of the sensory range. Everything appears butterscotch brown and has the texture of a ripe avocado. Walking the lighted paths of a commercial cavern may seem eerie, but wild caving through passageways seldom probed by cavers' lamps is an alien adventure. Forget easy locomotion—this is carb-burning work scrambling through the rocks. This cave is a 45-mile, multilevel maze with switchback tunnels and giant rooms. Advance registration is required for regular tours from November through April and for wild caving tours at any time; Organ Cave is open daily except Sunday.

To continue the driving tour, head northeast on WV 63 to its intersection with US 60 at Caldwell. (Warning: The underpass here has a 9-foot clearance. If your vehicle is taller, you will have to take US 219 to Lewisburg and then go right [east] on US 60 to Caldwell.) From here, our drive turns right toward White Sulphur Springs and The Greenbrier. But at this juncture, I heartily recommend a small side trip to the Greenbrier with the lowercase *t*—the river.

The Greenbriers: River & Resort

The waterway from which the famed resort derives its name is a few hundred yards to the west. Turn left on US 60, crossing the bridge and turning left into a parking area. This tiny park gives you the opportunity to hike the Greenbrier River Trail in its entirety. The path of RiverWise labyrinth traces the course of the Greenbrier River from its headwaters. The central path is the entire river. Environmental information and fun facts are posted at regular intervals over the 0.1-mile course. The area also features a native plant garden and children's play area as well as picnic tables.

Now that you know the lay of the land along the Greenbrier, go directly across US 60 to CR 38, Stone House Road, which travels 0.25 mile to the southern terminus of **Greenbrier River Trail State Park** (greenbrierrailtrail.com). You'll find a picnic area and restrooms here.

The Greenbrier River is one of the last few streams in this country to flow unimpeded by dams. Those who follow the trail from this spot north to Cass can experience some of the nation's finest smallmouth bass fishing, as well as pristine beauty and solitude.

At 78 miles, it is one of the longest rail-trails in the nation, snaking around the peaks of Marlin, Thorny Creek, and Thomas Mountains, past sleepy little villages with names such as Hopper, Stony Bottom, and Keister. The route is

RiverWise labyrinth recreates the path of the Greenbrier River at Caldwell.

interspersed with small farms, hemlock-shaded forest, and rhododendron-covered banks. In the early mornings, you can often see wood ducks and herons lifting off its quiet waters. The trail passes two state forests—Calvin Price and Seneca—and the Watoga and Cass Scenic Railroad State Parks. In fact, the trail is a West Virginia park in itself.

To continue the drive, head back over the US 60 bridge toward White Sulphur Springs, following rippling Howard's Creek through a commercial area and along The Greenbrier's golf course. You round a curve beside the famed underground bunker, where government officials would hide out in event of a nuclear attack. No longer a secret, the bunker is open for tours several times a week. If you like, you can drive through the main entrance of **The Greenbrier** resort (green brier.com) on the left and admire the grounds. Several eateries, golf courses, and the main dining room are open to day visitors as well as overnight guests.

The Greenbrier resort recently purchased the nation's oldest golf course, Oakhurst Links, also located in White Sulphur Springs. The Links was built in 1884 and features golf the way it was played 130 years ago. Players—often dressed in period clothes—rent hickory-shaft clubs and hit gutta-percha balls off tees fashioned from sand and water. The National Hickory Championship has been played at Oakhurst since 1998.

When you are ready to leave The Greenbrier, continue east on US 60 through town. Just past the business district, look for the **White Sulphur Springs National Fish Hatchery** (wsshatcheryfriends.org) on the left. One of three primary broodstock stations for rainbow trout in the nation, the facility features raceways seething with trout of various sizes. There's also a trout exhibit in the visitor center.

Golfers at historic Oakhurst Links play the old-fashioned way, with hickory clubs and sand tees.

The hatchery also raises freshwater mussels, which are vital in maintaining stream-water quality. Unfortunately about 70 percent of them are extinct, endangered, or in need of special protection. You can see them in a free guided tour, but you must schedule this a week in advance. The hatchery hosts a May fishing derby as well as an October Freshwater Folk Festival.

When you are ready to resume the drive, proceed west on US 60 a few more blocks to the intersection with WV 92 and turn left (north). The road leads through pretty farm country between Middle and Meadow Creek Mountains.

In the summer you may enjoy taking a 3-mile side trip to the Blue Bend swimming hole in Anthony Creek at the forest service's Blue Bend Campground. This is a beautiful spot with a rock beach and a deep blue waterhole. To get there, turn left (west) at Alvon, and go 3 miles to Blue Bend.

Lake Sherwood, about 15 miles north near Neola, offers another beautiful swimming opportunity on national forest land. The 156-acre lake has 2 sandy beaches, one on an island accessed by a footbridge. Boat and canoe rentals are also available.

Continue on WV 92 as the forest draws closer to the road. Several miles north of Neola, you'll see a sign and small parking lot for the **Allegheny Trail** (wvscenic trails.org). West Virginia's counterpart to the Appalachian Trail runs the length of the state—330 miles of backbone ridges and hollows, north–south through some of the state's wildest, prettiest territory. It passes close to the highway here on its way to Watoga State Park (watoga.com) and appears again in Canaan Valley (Scenic Route 9) before ending at the Pennsylvania border near Bruceton Mills.

Huntersville Anticline, sometimes called Devil's Backbone, is located outside of Huntersville.

About 16 miles from Neola, you turn left as WV 92 north merges with WV 39 west. Continue past the old mineral springs resort village of Minnehaha Springs to scenic Knapp's Creek. Just before the Knapp's Creek Bridge, look to your left. The huge arch of exposed sandstone, known as Huntersville Anticline or Devil's Backbone, is a dramatic part of Brown's Mountain anticline. The rock was folded as the mountains formed. In another mile, you're in the Huntersville, the northern terminus of our drive. From here you can go west 6 miles to Marlinton, the northern end of Scenic Route 18, or head up WV 28 about 18 miles to Cass and Scenic Route 16. If you turn around and follow WV 39 east, you'll end up in Lexington, Virginia, near I-81.

Appendix:
For More Information

For more information on lands and events, please contact the following agencies and organizations.

General Information

West Virginia Division of Tourism
Building 3, Suite 100
State Capital Complex
1900 Kanawha Blvd. E.
Charleston, WV 25305
(800) 225-5982, (304) 558-2200
wvtourism.com
The West Virginia Division of Tourism provides exemplary services for visitors and prospective visitors. Call them for information or to be directly connected toll-free with any state agency, including parks, forests, and wildlife management areas plus many privately owned facilities.

They will also help you plan your trip, answer questions, and provide maps and phone numbers. Do you want a list of rafting companies, the best time to see the autumn leaves at the New River Gorge, or the date the Feast of Ramson will be held in Richwood? Contact them by phone, US mail, or through their website, and they will help you out.

Route 1

Historic Bethany
Bethany College
Bethany, WV 26032
(304) 829-7285
bethanywv.edu

Homer Laughlin China Co.
800 Fiesta Dr.
Newell, WV 26050
(800) 452-4462; (304) 387-1300
fiestafactorydirect.com

Oglebay Resort & Conference Center
WV 88 North
Wheeling, WV 26003
(877) 436-1797
(304) 243-4000
oglebay.com

Weirton Chamber of Commerce
3200 Main St.
Weirton, WV 26062
(304) 748-7212
weirtonchamber.com

Wheeling Convention & Visitors Bureau
1401 Main St.
Wheeling, WV 26003
(304) 233-7709
wheelingcvb.com

Route 2

Grave Creek Mound Archaeological Complex
801 Jefferson Ave.
Moundsville, WV 26041
(304) 843-4128
wvculture.org/museum/gravecreekmod
.html

Marion County Convention & Visitors Bureau
110 Adams St.
Fairmont, WV 26554
(304) 368-1123
marioncvb.com

Palace of Gold
3759 McCreary's Ridge Rd.
Moundsville, WV 26041
(304) 843-1600
palaceofgold.com

West Augusta Historical Society
915 E. Main St.
Mannington, WV 26582
(304) 986-7053

West Virginia State Penitentiary Tours
818 Jefferson Ave.
Moundsville, VA 26041
(304) 845-6200
wvpentours.com

Route 3

Blennerhassett Island Historical State Park
137 Juliana St.
Parkersburg, WV 26101-5331
(304) 420-4800
wvstateparks.com/park/blennerhassett-
island-historical-state-park

Greater Parkersburg Convention & Visitors Bureau
350 7th St.
Parkersburg, WV 26101
(304) 428-1130
(800) 752-4982
greaterparkersburg.com

Ohio River Islands National Wildlife Refuge
3983 Waverly Rd.
Williamstown, WV 26187
(304) 375-2926
fws.gov/refuge/ohio_river_islands

Oil and Gas Museum
119 3rd St.
Parkersburg, WV 26102
(304) 485-5446
oilandgasmuseum.com

Sistersville City Hall
200 Diamond St.
Sistersville, WV 26175
(304) 652-6361

Wetzel County Chamber of Commerce
201 Main St.
PO Box 271
New Martinsville, WV 26155
(304) 455-3825
wetzelcountychamber.com

Route 4

Cathedral State Park
12 Cathedral Park Dr.
Aurora, WV 26705
(304) 735-3771
cathedralstatepark.com

Preston County Convention & Visitors Bureau
200 Main St.
Kingwood, WV 26537
(304) 329-4660
visitmountaineercountry.com/preston-county

Route 5

Fort Ashby
227 Dans Run Rd.
Fort Ashby, WV 26719
(304) 298-3319
wvculture.org/history/settlement/fortashby02.html

Potomac Eagle Railroad
149 Eagle Dr.
Romney, WV 26757
(304) 424-0736
potomaceagle.com

Route 6

Berkeley Springs State Park
2 S. Washington St.
Berkeley Springs, WV 25411
(304) 258-2711
(800) CALL WVA
wvstateparks.com/park/berkeley-springs-state-park

Chesapeake & Ohio Canal National Historic Park
Hancock Visitor Center
439 E. Main St.
Hancock, MD 21750
(301) 739-4200
nps.gov/choh

Travel Berkeley Springs CVB
127 Fairfax St.
Berkeley Springs, WV 25411
(800) 447-8797
berkeleysprings.com

Route 7

Harpers Ferry National Historic Park
PO Box 65, 171 Shoreline Dr.
Harpers Ferry, WV 25425
(304) 535-6029
nps.gov/hafe

Jefferson County Convention & Visitors Bureau
37 Washington Crt.
Harpers Ferry, WV 25425
(304) 535-2627
(866) HELLO WV
discoveritallwv.com

Martinsburg/Berkeley County Convention & Visitors Bureau
126 E. Race St.
Martinsburg, WV 25401
(304) 264-8801
(800) 498-2386
travelwv.com

Rumsey Steamboat Museum
c/o O'Hurley's General Store
205 E. Washington St.
Shepherdstown, WV 25443
(304) 876-6907
ohurley.com

Route 8

Buckhannon/Upshur Convention & Visitors Bureau
14 Main St.
Buckhannon, WV 26201
(304) 473-1400
visitbuckhannon.org

Philippi Convention & Visitor Bureau
108 Main St.
Philippi, WV 26416
(304) 457-3700, ext. 211
Philippi CVB on Facebook

Swiss Village of Helvetia
Helvetia, WV 26224
(304) 924-6435
helvetiawv.com

West Virginia Wildlife Center
PO Box 38, State Route 20
French Creek, WV 26218
(304) 924-6211
wvdnr.gov/wildlife/wildlifecenter.shtm

Route 9

Blackwater Falls State Park
PO Drawer 490
1584 Blackwater Lodge Road (CR 29)
Davis, WV 26260
(304) 259-5216
wvstateparks.com/park/blackwater-falls-state-park

Canaan Valley National Wildlife Refuge
6263 Appalachian Hwy.
Davis, WV 26260
(304) 866-3858
fws.gov/refuge/canaan_valley

Canaan Valley Resort & Conference Center
230 Main Lodge Rd.
Davis, WV 26260
(304) 866-4121
canaanresort.com

Route 10

Hardy County Historical Society
122 N. Main St.
Moorefield, WV 26836
(304) 257-3844
visithardy.com/listing/hardy-county-historical-society

The Nature Conservancy
West Virginia Chapter
(304) 634-0160
nature.org/en-us/about-us/where-we-work/united-states/west-virginia/

Route 11

Lost River State Park
321 Park Dr.
Mathias, WV 26812
(304) 897-5372
(800) 225-5982
wvstateparks.com/park/lost-river-state-park

Routes 12, 13 & 14

US Forest Service Monongahela National Forest Forest Headquarters
200 Sycamore St.
Elkins, WV 26241
(304) 636-1800
elkinsandandolphwv.com/place/monongahela-national-forest-headquarters/

US Forest Service Monongahela National Forest Seneca Rocks Visitor Center
PO Box 13, WV-28
Seneca Rocks, WV 26884
(304) 567-2827
wvtourism.com/company/seneca-rocks-discovery-center/

Route 15

Monongahela National Forest Marlinton Ranger District
PO Box 210
Marlinton, WV 24954
(304) 799-4334
fs.usda.gov/mnf

Monongahela National Forest Gauley Ranger District
PO Box 110
Richwood, WV 26261
(304) 846-2695
fs.usda.gov/mnf

Richwood Area Chamber of Commerce
PO Box 267; 38 Edgewood Ave.
Richwood, WV 26261
(304) 846-6790
richwoodchamberofcommerce.org

West Virginia Rails-to-Trails Council for Cranberry Tri-River Rail Trail
wvrailtrails.org

Route 16

Cass Scenic Railroad State Park
12363 Cass Rd.
Cass, WV 24927
(304) 636-9477
wvstateparks.com/park/cass-scenic-railroad

Durbin & Greenbrier Valley Railroad
315 Railroad Ave.
Elkins, WV 26241
(304) 636-9477
mountainrailwv.com

Green Bank
PO Box 2, 155 Observatory Rd.
Green Bank, WV 24944
(304) 456-2150
greenbankobservatory.org

Snowshoe Mountain Resort
10 Snowshoe Dr.
Snowshoe, WV 26209
(304) 572-1000
(877) 441-8386
snowshoemtn.com

Route 17

Fayetteville Convention & Visitors Bureau
310 N. Court St.
Fayetteville, WV 25840
(304) 574-1500
visitfayettevillewv.com

National Park Service
New River Gorge National River
Canyon Rim Visitor Center
162 Visitor Center Rd.
Lansing, WV 25862
(304) 574-2115
nps.gov/neri

National Park Service New River
Gorge National River Headquarters
104 Main St.
Thurmond, WV 25936
(304) 465-0508
nps.gov/neri

Route 18

Droop Mountain Battlefield State Park
HC 64 Box 189
Hillsboro WV 24946
(304) 653-4254
wvstateparks.com/park/droop-mountain-battlefield-state-park

Greenbrier County Convention & Visitors Bureau
905 W. Washington St.
Lewisburg, WV 24901
(800) 833-2068
(304) 645-1000
greenbrierwv.com

Lost World Caverns
907 Lost World Rd.
Lewisburg, WV 24901
(304) 645-6677
lostworldcaverns.com

Monongahela National Forest
Marlinton Ranger District
PO Box 210
Marlinton, WV 24954
(304) 799-4334
fs.usda.gov/mnf

Pocahontas County Convention & Visitors Bureau
301 8th Street
Marlinton, WV 24954
(304) 799-4636
pocahontascountywv.com

Watoga State Park & Greenbrier River Trail State Park
Seebert Rd. (CR 27-3)
Marlinton, WV 24954
(304) 799-4087
(800) CALL WVA
wvstateparks.com/park/watoga

Route 19

Amtrak
(800) 872-7245
amtrak.com

Thurmond Depot Visitor Center
(304) 465-8550 seasonally
nps.gov/neri

Route 20

**Tug Valley Chamber of Commerce
Coal House**
73 2nd Avenue
PO Box 376
Williamson, WV 25661
(304) 235-5240
tugvalleychamber.com

Route 21

Bluestone State Park
Bluestone Park Rd.
Nimitz, WV 25978
(304) 466-2805
(800) 225-5982
wvstateparks.com/park/bluestone-state-park

Organ Cave
242 Organ Cave Dr..
Ronceverte, WV 24970
(304) 645-7600
organcave.com

Pipestem Resort State Park
3405 Pipestem Knob Rd.
Pipestem, WV 25979
(304) 466-1800
(800) 225-5982
wvstateparks.com/park/pipestem-resort-state-park

Route 22

**Monroe County Tourism Information
Center**
PO Box 238
Union, WV 24983
(304) 772-3003, ext 15
travelmonroe.com

Route 23

City of Welch
Welch Municipal Building
88 Howard St.
Welch, WV 24801
(304) 436-3113

Coal Heritage Trail Association
PO Box 15
100 Kelly Ave.
Oak Hill, WV 25901
(304) 465-3720
coalheritage.org

**Mercer County Convention & Visitors
Bureau**
704 Bland St.
Bluefield, WV 24701
(304) 325-8438
(800) 223-3206
visitmercercounty.com

**Southern West Virginia Convention &
Visitors Bureau**
1408 Harper Rd.
Beckley, WV 25801
(304) 252-2244
(800) VISIT WV
visitwv.com

Tamarack
1 Tamarack Dr.
Beckley, WV 25801
(304) 256-6843
88-TAMARACK
tamarackwv.com

Twin Falls Resort State Park
Bear Hole Rd (CR 4-1)
Mullens, WV 25882
(304) 294-4000
(800) CALL WVA
wvstateparks.com/park/twin-falls-
resort-state-park

Route 24

Babcock State Park
486 Babcock Rd.
Clifftop, WV 25831
(304) 438-3004
(800) CALL WVA
wvstateparks.com/park/babcock-state-
park

Hawks Nest State Park
49 Hawks Nest Heights Rd.
Ansted, WV 25812
(304) 658-5212
(800) CALL WVA
wvstateparks.com/park/hawks-nest-
state-park

**Midland Trail Scenic Highway
Association**
237 Capitol St.
Charleston, WV 25301
(304) 343-6001
(800) 7688360
midlandtrail.com

Route 25

**Greenbrier County Convention &
Visitors Bureau**
905 Washington St.
Lewisburg, WV 24901
(800) 833-2068
(304) 645-1000
greenbrierwv.com

Organ Cave
242 Organ Cave.
Ronceverte, WV 24970
(304) 645-7600
organcave.com

Index